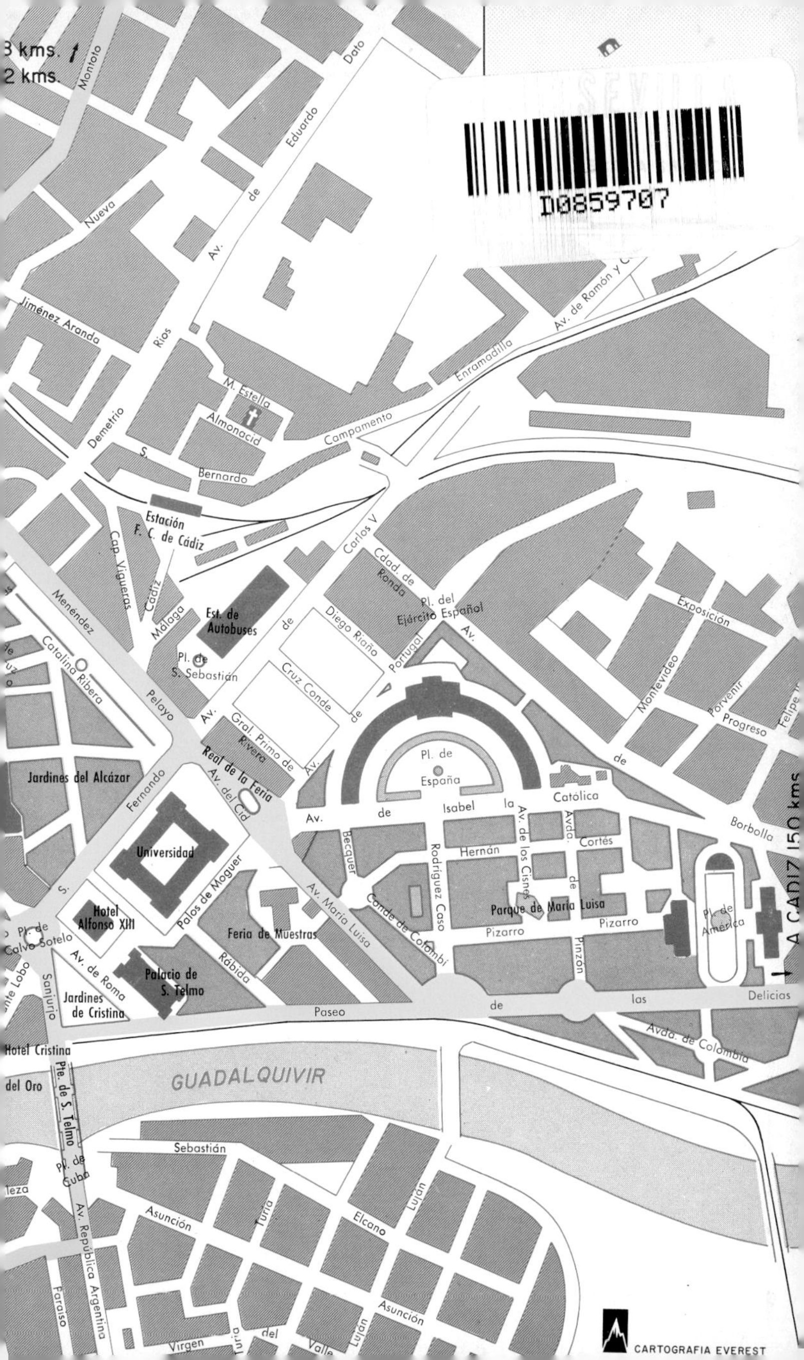

3 kms.
2 kms.
Montoto
Dato
Eduardo
Av. de Eduardo Dato
Nueva
Jiménez Aranda
Demetrio Ríos
Av. de Ramón y Ca...
Enramadilla
M. Estella
Almonacid
Campamento
S. Bernardo
Estación F. C. de Cádiz
Carlos V
Cap. Vigueras
Cádiz
Málaga
Est. de Autobuses
Pl. de S. Sebastián
Menéndez Pelayo
Catalina Ribera
Cdad. de Ronda
Pl. del Ejército Español
Diego Riaño
Cruz Conde
Av. de Portugal
Exposición
Montevideo
Porvenir
Progreso
Felipe II
Gral. Primo de Rivera
Real de la Feria
Av. del Cid
Pl. de España
Jardines del Alcázar
S. Fernando
Universidad
Av. de Isabel la Católica
Av. de los Cisnes
Avda. Hernán Cortés
Becquer
Rodríguez Caso
Borbolla
A CADIZ 150 kms.
Palos de Moguer
Av. María Luisa
Conde de Colombí
Parque de María Luisa
Pizarro
Pinzón
Pl. de América
Hotel Alfonso XIII
Feria de Muestras
Pl. de Calvo Sotelo
Av. de Roma
Rábida
Palacio de S. Telmo
Sanjurio
Jardines de Cristina
Paseo de las Delicias
Avda. de Colombia
Hotel Cristina
del Oro
GUADALQUIVIR
Pte. de S. Telmo
Sebastián
Pl. de Cuba
Av. República Argentina
Asunción
Turia
Elcano
Luján
Paraíso
Virgen del Valle
CARTOGRAFIA EVEREST

«Giralda, the mother of artists, the mold for bull fighters». →

Impreso en España. Printed in Spain. León-1972

ISBN 84-241-4383-3
Depósito Legal-LE-764 /1972

Litografía EVEREST - Carret. León-Astorga, Km. 4,500 - LEON

SEVILLE

Text: MANUEL BENDALA LUCOT.

Photographs: Archivo Mas.
Oronoz.
Paisajes Españoles.
Graphic Archive of the Ministry of Information and Tourism.
Sicilia.
Cifra Gráfica.
Cubiles.
Arribas.
FISA.
Provincial Archaeological Museum.
Ruiz-Vernacci.
J. Pato, (c.) Blanco y Negro.
Manuel Acosta.

Translation: DIORKI.-MADRID.

CUARTA EDICION

EDITORIAL EVEREST

Apartado 339 - LEÓN (ESPAÑA)

THE GIRALDA

It can never be repeated too many times: the Giralda is Andalusian and not African; it belongs to Seville and not to the Orient. Roman and Visigothic stones formed the foundation of this minaret, homage paid by the African victor to the city that won his heart. And he was so taken with the art of Andalusia that he filled his homeland with bricklayers from Seville; many of the notable and beautiful things that remain in Morocco from the medieval period were done by Spanish Moors.

Tradition says that a Moor from Seville, called Gever or Guever, was the architect for the Giralda. From a legend in the Historia de Fez, known in 1805, later autohors affirm that the construction of the great synagogue and its minaret was ordered by Abu Ya' qub Yusuf in the year 1171 (567 of the Hegira) and begun by the architect Ahman Ibn Baso.

The Mohammedan historian Abdel Kalin wrote: «Almanzor Jacob, successor to his father Jucef Jacub, after great victories, returned triumphant to Seville and ordered finished the work on the great synagogue and the lofty tower, and the beautiful apple, that was so big that there was no other like it, and whose diameter was such that, to get it through the door, it was necessary to remove the stone of the threshold; while this was being done in Spain, the order continued for the construction of the fortress in Morocco and the one in Rabat».

The victor of Alarcos entrusted the inspection of the work to the poet Abubequer Benzoar, and this is how the Giralda became a ballad or a devotional verse («saeta»). Ali de Gomara was in charge of the brick work; 87 feet up, he began to make lace-like designs —«axaracas»— with «aximeces» on the outside and thirty five ramps on the inside, so that fifty years later Fernando III could ride up on horseback. The tower was 250 feet high and «was crowned by four spheres, one on top of the other, in gilt bronze, whose brilliance could be seen eight leagues away», according to Alfonso X.

An earthquake knocked the spheres down and the tower remained cut off until 1568 when Hernán Ruiz raised it another 100 feet, with four Renaissance bodies and the gigantic Triumph of the Faith at the top. Because this turned around when the wind hit the banner, the people called it the «giralda» or weathervane, which is a beautiful name for «this African made tower of admirable sorrow» that was, and still is, the most graceful belfrey in all of Christendom.

«Seville is a tower / full of fine treasures».

THE VIEW FROM THE GIRALDA

The incline of the ramps is not steep. «The windows are not all on the same level on the four sides, because they are placed in such a way that there is one at each landing, so that when one stops to rest during the climb, he can look out at the street». There was an obvious touristic interest in the construction of the tower: the Moorish chiefs wanted their subjects to climb slowly in order to contemplate, with an increasingly greater view, the movement on the dock, the grace of the residencial area, the green of the farms with the hills in the distance.

Once past the bells, 93 meters up, we can see the urban landscape that is no longer one of low, variegated roof tops, broken by multicolored domes and towers. The four high balconies directly face the four points of the compass.

Fifteen years ago the city ended, to the East, at the Ronda de Capuchinos, then, the plain toward Carmona... Today the urban landscape is extended with a belt of new neighborhoods and the wall of the Polígono de San Pablo, the most ambicious official work in the face of the housing problem.

To the South, the small Nervio, the anarchical Hill of the Águila and the recent Labor University, with the plain toward Alcalá and Dos Hermanas. The horizon is closed today by the new city which has sprung up behind the Tamarguillo, the backbone of forced flooding. And behind the towers of the Plaza de España and the foliage of the Park, the new groups are leaving the charms of the Porvenir and Heliopolis in the shadows.

To the West, the Giralda overlooks the Bull Ring, the river, Triana with its permanent black streaks in the chimneys, the other river and the high line of the Aljarafe. Today, the embankment that filled in the river, the new Triana, Los Remedios and, at the back, topping the Cuesta, the purification plant in El Carambolo, a provision for the thirst of Gran Seville, with a population of more than one million. To the North, with the river as the boundary and the Cartuja, the landscape has not changed.

There was a classic definition: «Table olives can be seen from the Giralda». Today, with eternal Seville at its feet, from the Giralda it is even difficult to see the magic silver of the olive trees.

← «Seville —air of light and air of aroma—».

A view from the Giralda. →

The view from the Giralda.

The weather vane, crowning the Giralda.

THE CATHEDRAL

In 1921, when the civil buildings did not compete with the Gothic spires and the Plateresque belfries, a Portuguese wrote: «The Cathedral is that Gothic structure that, finding shelter in the cornered Arab tower and fortified in its surroundings by the bulwarks of the Renaissance, is seen from far away, moving and trim, like the fluctuating peak of the houses of the city. Because from far away and from everywhere, the immense, firm structure looks like a fantastic galley, carrying the Giralda like a figurehead and sailing on a sea full of small vessels and launches».

A lovely definition, a lovely image. One can, still today, stand at some distant point or on the flat roofs of the Plaza de Cuba and be impressed with this image of grandeur. After a time, the spaces began to close in, nearby buildings were constructed and the vistas became cut off; in an attempt to somewhat free the view of the Cathedral, they agreed to a timid widening of the avenue. There was even a plan to form a large plaza in front of the west side, but they lost their first chance when they allowed the National Institute of Social Welfare to be built.

If sixteen years ago they had thought with the criteria of today, with a view to tourism, it might have been possible to soon —within another three or four hard rainy winters— have the western side visually unobstructed, and the Cathedral adjusted to its landscape.

A door on the south —Lonja— San Cristóbal or of the Princes, was done in 1895; three on the north, Lagarto —old— and Concepcion, which is so new that it was inaugurated in 1917; these lead to the Patio of the Oranges, and San Fernando, done in 1660, which leads to the Sacrarium; and the very old, original doors: two on the east —Plaza of Our Lady of the Kings— Little Bells and Sticks, and the three on the west: Major, Baptism and St. Miguel. If one could take them all in with one glance, from the foundation to the sky, with the 160 meters of façade, any Christian would think to himself just what one of the members of the Cathedral council proposed at the beginning of the XV century: «Let us build a church in such a way that those who see it will think we are crazy».

Seville. Cathedral. Detail of the entrance of the Campanillas.

Cathedral. Tympanum of the entrance of the Nacimiento and detail of the entrance to the baptistery.

Cathedral. Detail of the interior

A SYMPHONY OF CHISELS

More than one hundred years, day by day —1402 to 1519, counting the immediate reconstruction of the fallen dome—, the stonecutters were placing and working stone on stone in a symphonic revelry of chisels and hammars. Art and crafts from two centuries left an indelible mark in the grand marvel that is this temple of Christianity —the third in the world— and in all the grace of its structure, reaching the synthesis, not of a nation at its highest, but rather of an empire that seemed enough for the Common Market of today. French-Gothic structure by an unknown architect, where we also find the ingenious of Flemish, Germans, Italians, Hebrews and an unending legion of genius and skill from all the kingdoms of Spain.

Lines written in praise of the Cathedral would extend for miles, but we must also proclaim its majestic immensity, the harmony of its proportions —116 meters long and 76 wide—, the miracle of its 68 high domes, held up on the light branches that originate in 40 pillars, as a delight to the eyes in their successive unions and harmonious movements. Here doors, pointed arches, clay baked in the fire of faith and glazed by time, chapels, genuine railings in Plateresque wrought iron, alabasters, crackling flames of light from ninety-three stained glass windows, a dazzling group of figures and decoration in sculptures and altar pieces accumulated by twenty generations, choir chairs...

The largest altarpiece in the Christian world, «the one with the richest, finest and most abundant ornament known in the Gothic style», is two hundred and twenty square meters large with more than a thousand figures in a summary of Sacred History. Masters of various nationalities —not less than twenty-six— were successively working on the altarpiece, beginning with the Flemish Dancart and ending with Juan Bautista Vázquez, from 1482 to 1564.

The Cathedral of Seville, the tomb of many famous men, preserves the body, intact, of the Holy Conqueror of the city, a symbol of all human virtues, «the most loyal and the most true and the most frank, and the most enterprising, and the most elegant and the most illustrious and the most suffering, and the most humble», according to the epitaph written in Latin, Arabic, Hebrew and Spanish. Fernando III was the Great Lord of the people living together.

Cathedral. Main Altarpiece. →

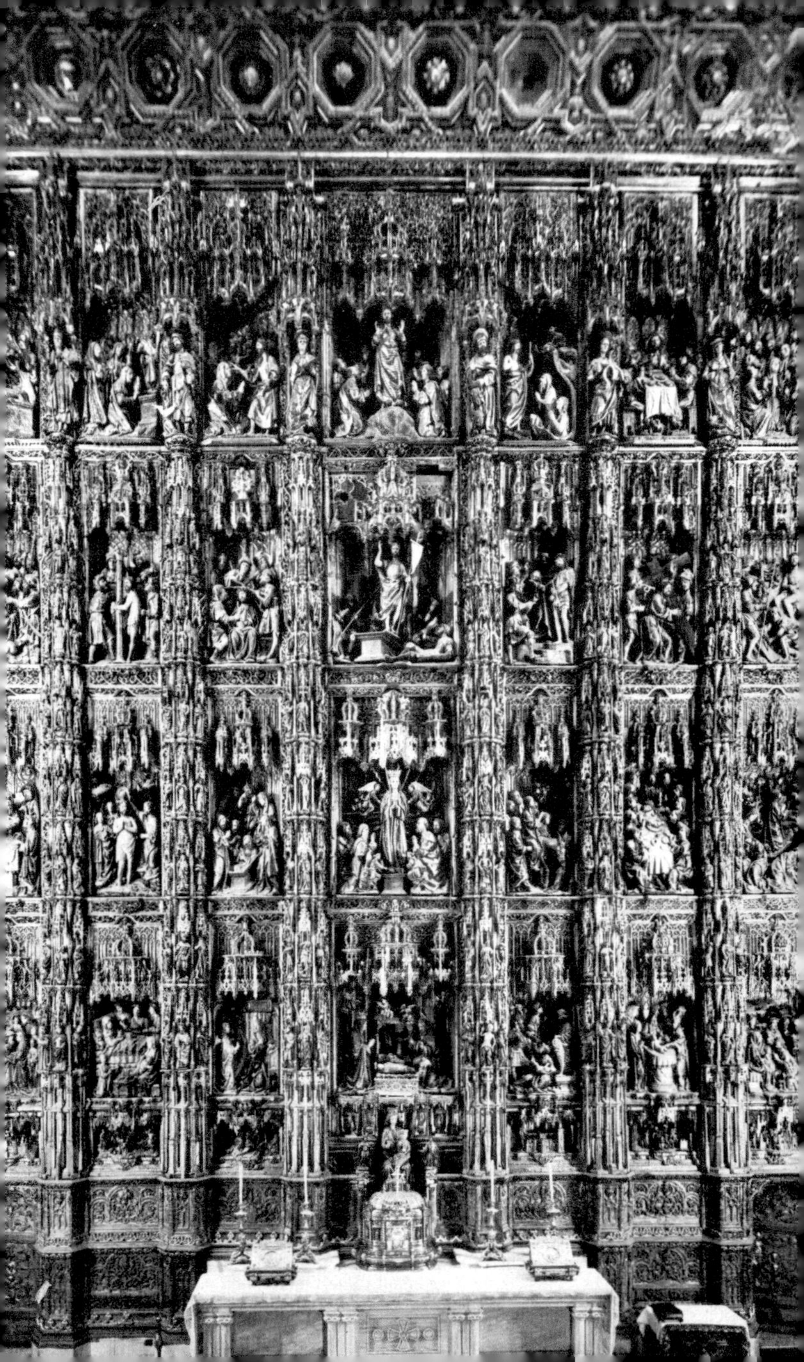

Cathedral. Central wrought iron work of the Main Chapel.

Cathedral. High Sacristy. The Purification of the Virgin by Alejo Fernández. →

Cathedral. Sacristy of the Chalices. Christ of the Clemency by Martínez Montañés.

Cathedral. Chapel of San Hermenegildo. Tomb of the cardenal Cervantes, by Lorenzo Mercadante. →

Cathedral. Chapel of Escalas. Glazed Terra cota representing the Virgin of Granada, by Andrea della Robbia.

← Aerial view of the Cathedral of Seville.

← Cathedral. Sword of San Fernando.

INSIDE THE CATHEDRAL

It took 120 years to build the structure; and three hundred years more to fill it. Five centuries of artists contributed to this magnificence.

Juan Norman was the architect until 1472; then Pedro de Toledo, Francisco Rodríguez and Juan Hoces, until 1496; Simón until 1502, and then Alfonso Rodríguez and Gonzalo de Rosas, who closed the dome. The reconstruction of this fell to Pedro López, Enrique de Egeas and Juan de Álava, and Juan Gil de Hontañón was commissioned to carry out the plans and he finished it. Diego de Riaño and Martín de Gainza designed the Gothic sacristy of the Chalices. Gainza also planned the royal chapel, where we find the Plateresque part of the Cathedral, but it was finished by Juan de Maeda, a disciple of Siloe in 1575. The Plateresque design of the main sacristy and the Renaissance design of the capitular room belonged to Riaño. These plans were accepted after presenting them before a contest board; such a formality was not demanded of Miguel de Zumárraga for the parish of the Sagrario, «a work which begins the plague of the Greco-Roman decline in the cathedral».

The windows were painted, beginning in 1504, by Micer Cristóbal Alemán, Juan Jaques, Juan Bernal, Vivan and Bernardino de Gelandia, being followed, between 1525 and 1557, by Arnao de Flandes and Arnao de Vergara. They were finished in 1569 by Carlos Bruges and Vicente Menandro. The railings were by fray Francisco de Salamanca, fray Juan, Antonio de Palencia, Sancho Muñoz, Juan de Yepes, Esteban and Diego Idobro. The choir chairs are a work of Nufro Sánchez, finished by Dancart. The large monstrance, «the largest and the best piece in silver of its kind known to exist», according to Arfe, its creator. The Tenebrae —an immense candelabrum with a triangular head— and the lecturn are by Bartolomé Morel.

The sculptures that Lorenzo Mercadante de Bretaña and Pedro Millán did for the west doors, and Miguel Perrín —70 years later— for the east doors, are of baked clay. Of the first ones, we have the tomb of the cardenal Cervantes, the two Santiagos and the Virgin of the Pillar. Andrea della Robbia is included with two lovely terra cotas, the Virgin of the Cushion and the Virgin of Granada. In the sacristy of the Chalices, the Christ of Clemency, a masterpiece by Martínez Montañés. The Tomb of the archbishop Hurtado de Mendoza, by Domenico Alessandro Fancelli, and the grand one of Christopher Columbus, by Arturo Mérida, one of the last examples of Romantic statuary (1891).

And all the painters, Sturmio, Pedro de Campaña, Roelas, Luis de Vargas, Herrera el Mozo, Murillo, Zurbarán, Valdés Leal, Alejo Fernández, Alonso Cano and many, many more.

Cathedral. Chapel of Pilar. Image of Our Lady, by Pedro Millán; the Virgin of the Old, in the chapel of the same name.

Cathedral. Chapel of the Old. Tomb of the cardenal Hurtado de Mendoza, by Domenico Fancelli.

Cathedral. Chapel of San Antonio. Vision of St. Anthony of Padua, by Murillo.

Cathedral. Tomb of Christopher Columbus, by Arturo Mélida (XIX c.) and the St. Christopher by Pérez de Alesio (XVI c.).

Cathedral. Interior of the main sacristy.

Cathedral. Main Sacristy. Monstrance by Juan de Arfe,
and the Descent by Pedro de Campaña.

Cathedral. Capitular room.

← Cathedral. Main Sacristy. Alfonso tablets, relicary triptych from the XIII century.

← Cathedral. Ornament room. Standard of Fernando III the Saint.

Cathedral. Royal chapel. Detail of the tomb of Alfonso X the Wise.

Cathedral. Chapel of the Mariscal. Painting of the patrons, by Pedro de Campaña.

Cathedral. The marvelous Inmaculada, by Montañés, in the chapel of the Little Comception.

← Cathedral. Three details of the choir chairs.

THE FORTRESSES AND THE ALCÁZAR OF THE KING DON PEDRO

The homes of the great Moslem lords —the palaces, and on a smaller scale, those that weren't— were divided into three areas: for public life, for private life and the walk or garden.

Of the Arab fortresses —probably al Mu'tadid, enriched by several «abbasita» kingdoms and later by the Almohade Moors— there remain the beautiful walled enclosure that extended toward the river —the Tower of Abbdelazis, the Tower of Silver and the Tower of Gold— and the Patio of Plaster. Barracks, warehouses, palaces and other buildings were destroyed by earthquakes and fires, or they were absorbed into later constructions or taken apart by the reforms of Carlos I, Felipe IV and Fernando VII and Isabel II.

We can get an idea of the pleasantness and comfort of Arab fortresses from the fact that Abu Yusuf Ya'qub, wounded in Santarem, did not return to his native Morocco and that Fernando III —until his death—, Alfonso X, Sancho IV and Alfonso XI, on the pretext of continuing the Reconquest, all had their court here.

Pedro I of Castilla, respecting as much as he could everything that fell into his hands, built the most marvelous example of Christian-Moorish art.

The king Don Pedro slept very little and worked a lot, with the hope of perhaps being able to enjoy some peace in the wonderful Alcázar that he had built, which was finished in 1366.

In the second part of the sumptuous façade, there is a large epigraphic frieze that repeats eight times in «cufico» characters: «There is no victor but Allah», in interesting contrast to the Gothic letters which tell us of the one who ordered the construction of the building. Around the great Patio of the Maidens, there are three reception rooms: the one for Embassadors, in front, on whose doors, African characters sing praises to «our lord the Sultan, exalted, Don Pedro, king of Castilla and León», the so called Bedroom of the Moorish Kings, to the right, where we can read «glory to our lord the Sultan Don Pedro. May Allah help and protect him», and to the left, the one that has received the name of the Room of Carlos V, because its magnificent panelling was done in times of the emperor.

The intimate life of the palace was held around the Patio of the Dolls, but the clumsy names given to the various rooms do not really give us a fair idea of what it was like.

Panelling, «sebcas», tile inlays, bows, Mozarabic details and many other things that were worked, woven and drawn for a man who never rested by Christian and Islamic masters from Seville, Granada, Toledo and Córdoba.

Alcázar. Main façade of the palace of Pedro I. →

Alcázar. The marvelous Patio of the Maidens.

Alcázar. Detail of the Patio of Dolls.

Alcázar. Detail of the tapestry of the War of Túnez (XVI c.). →

Gardens of the Alcázar. «Under the pure grace of the sky of Seville...».

THE GARDENS OF THE ALCÁZAR

The third part of Moslem life was the garden. The idea that «water hides tears» was an invention of our Moslems, and until a short while ago —with the exception of El Retiro, La Granja and Aranjuez— all the famous gardens of Spain were of Moorish or Christian-Moorish design: Alhambra, Generalife, Alcazaba in Almería, those in Valencia and Murcia, the palm tree gardens in Elche, etc.

The gardens of the Alcázar in Seville are a delight, in spite of everything. If they had only been preserved in the way that Rodrigo Caro described them in the XVII century...! And by that time the Emperor has placed his Christian-Moorish pavillion there. Soon after, they installed the Neo-classical one of the Grotesque, which Felipe V remodeled to his own taste.

The kingdoms of Seville and the Almohade Moors made and perfected the ingenious and intelligent work of bringing water from Alcalá de Guadaira —16 kilometers away and an aqueduct, that until now has been poorly called «Los Caños de Carmona»— with the sole purpose of watering the gardens of the palaces; and it was so perfect that, with hardly a single reform, it provided the drinking water for the capital until 1948. A garden fed by all the water that served to extinguish the thirst of the people of Seville, until they numbered more than 300,000.

The various gardens of the Alcázar, are today called «of the Pond», with the gallery of grotesques; «of the Dance»; «of the Bath of doña María de Padilla», whose subterranean galleries are from the XVI century; «of the Grotto»; «of the Prince or of the bananas»; «Large Garden», with a XVII century entrance; «of the Lion», whose old orange trees delighted the «Navaggiero» Embassador; «of the Pavillion of Carlos V»; «of the Laberinth», rebuilt in a different place, thanks to a plan drawn in a tile in the pavillion; and those that still have no name because they are of recent construction, according to English or natural taste. In 1913, and as an approach to the new gardens taken from the Huerta de El Retiro, they set up the gate of the palace of the Dukes of Arcos, of Marchena, which is an archaeological gem from the end of the XV century, at the point of disappearing because of its state of ruin. The Plaza Mayor of Marchena is at present being restored and it is probable that this gate will return to its original location.

In the Alcázar, we find old gardens, Renaissance, Baroque, XVIII century and modern ones. But the orange and lemon trees, the myrtle, the lady of night and the jazmin, the tile inlays and the sound of the water continue to make us think «I have the soul of the tuberose of the Spanish Arab».

Alcázar. The Virgin of the Navegators, by Alejo Fernández. →

Alcázar. Altar of tiles, by Niculoso Pisano in the Oratory of the Catholic Kings.

Alcázar. Room of the Embassadors. →

Alcázar. Detail of the plaster frieze in one of the rooms next to the Room of Embassadors.

Alcázar. Patio of Dolls.

«The water whispers eternally in the patio».

Alcázar. Pavillion of Carlos V in the Gardens.

THE NEIGHBORHOOD OF SANTA CRUZ

It is not difficult to define a monument or a landscape, but it is to define a sector, the Neighborhood of Santa Cruz. This sector is in the very center of Seville. It borders on the Alcázar, the gardens of Murillo and Catalina Ribera, and the streets Mateos Gago, Fabiola and Santa María la Blanca. All in all, just a little square. With the long strides of the Northmen, we could cover the area in a quarter of an hour. This neighborhood must have something when no one takes less than three hours to see it; and there have been those who have gone in when the night was young and come out just as the sun was hitting the top of the Giralda.

We enter the sector —well, no, we don't enter really— because the first thing we must do is cross the little Plaza of Santa Marta. We approach and are surprised; we sit down with a friend on a stone bench; all of Becquer's poems or Heine's come rushing to mind, and then, very quietly, we get up and leave. Then we can enter the neighborhood, perhaps by way of a street that has recently been opened between the walls of the Alcázar and the Palacio de la Diputación; six years ago, this spot was mysteriously occupied by the house of an antique collector. Because of this fact, the wall has been discovered intact, and very beautiful; and we reach the Plaza of the Alianza. The classical way is to enter through the Patio de Banderas; it is like a Plaza Mayor in Castilla, but in Andalusian style; an arch of walls to enter, two-story houses with balconies and gay colors, orange trees in the center, the balconies of the Alcaide in front and the arch of Judería, as we continue with our itinerary.

We reach the «Callejón del Agua» or Alley of Water by way of the arch of Judería. In bright daylight or under a full moon we can see that the post cards of streets and plazas —Vida, Jamerdana, Justino de Neve, Pimienta, Cruces, Mezquita, Lope de Rueda, Santa Teresa, Doña Elvira— are pale in comparison, even though they are printed in beautiful technicolor. Camilo Mauclair, half a century ago, confessed that time had stopped. Then, the Plaza de Santa Cruz, with the cross of Cerrajería, a wrought iron work from 1692, which has been located here since 1918, and the gay houses and the severe plaque dedicated to Murillo.

Two steps away, the Plaza de Alfaro, with a palm tree inside a balcony, the walls of the Alcázar in the corner and a couple of palaces leaning over to look into the gardens. A staircase, and perhaps there is still time to contemplate the moon or measure the unbelievable narrowness of a street with our arms...

A corner of the Neighborhood of Santa Cruz. →

Street of the Descalzos.

← The Patio of Banderas.

In the neighborhood of Santa Cruz, as in all of Seville, «whereever you look, the Giralda».

The charming plaza of Doña Elvira.

Church of the Hospital of the Venerable Fathers. Dome of the presbytery, painted by Valdés Leal.

Church of Santa María la Blanca. The Last Supper, by Murillo.

THE VENERABLE ONES

The first famous comedian —and author— who travelled throughout the rather recently united Iberian territory with his company of players was Lope de Rueda, a native of Seville; his name has been given to a street near the scene of his triumphs: the Corral de Doña Elvira. At the same time, «Doña Elvira» is the most typical of all the plazas in Seville. It was reformed in 1924 to give it its present appearance, which today suffers a small variation: the ground floor is dedicated to the tourist business with souvenirs, ceramics, embroidered goods and general crafts.

In 1698, on top of the authentic Corral de Comedias de Doña Elvira, —after twenty-two years of plays directed by Leonardo de Figueroa— they built the Hospital of the Venerable Fathers, whose church was the first to be dedicated to St. Fernando, because its inauguration coincided with the canonization of the monarch. The Venerable Ones offers famous pieces and is perhaps an interesting stop on our tour through the Neighborhood of Santa Cruz.

Its patio, in «Sevillano» style —we shall talk more of this later— has the special feature in that its galleries of arches begin at a higher level than the patio itself, in the center of which there is an original lower fountain, surrounded by five wide stairs.

The inside of its church, in Greco-Roman style with one single nave, is one of the most perfect examples of Baroque. The brushes of Juan Valdés Leal and of his son and disciple Lucas Valdés, in addition to those of other interesting signatures, left their mark, in all their dimension and mastery, on the plaster of domes, vaults and walls, and on several notable canvases.

In 1965, the Permanent Exposition of the Treasure of the «Cofradías» (Holy Week organizations) of Seville became installed in the Venerable Ones. It occupies the rooms of the ground floor which had, until then, been used for formal weddings. Attached to the walls, out in the open or in twenty-seven glass cases, there are exhibited —in constant renovation— the static, motionless examples of the processional treasure that become bursting with life during the days of Holy Week. Here we find the canopies, the flies, the long poles, the ventilators, the side skirts, the candelabra, the cloak, the crown, the vases of flowers and the candels that miraculously take our breaths away when a Virgin, swaying from the shoulders of her porters, passes down a narrow street.

On the edge of the old Jewish sector, we find the church of Santa María la Blanca which contains some unbelievably somber work by Murillo. And the erudites are of the opinion that beneath the Baroque covering of the Borja brothers, there is, intact, the only nave of the synagogue that existed as it was until 1391.

Street of the Pimienta: «The alley is a wound / deep and cured with lime».

The plaza of Santa Cruz, in the neighborhood of the same name.

Complete aerial view of the plaza de España and a partial view of Seville.

Archive of the Indies. Map of Tetela, a native town in New Spain.

The plaza de América.

THE ARCHIVE OF THE INDIES

In the XVI century, the merchants of Seville were in the habit of carrying out their transactions, shouting, in the Patio of Oranges or on the steps of the Cathedral. But when the sun beat down fiercely or when it was cold or when it poured rain, they continued their business within the Cathedral...

When the merchants of Seville were thrown out of the temple for the last time, the archbishop himself, Sandoval y Rojas, used all his influence with Felipe II to have a special place built which would be worthy of such an important matter. He realized how vital the mercantile business was, since Seville was the port of the Indies. The request was made in 1572, when the name of Herrera had already begun to sound in the works of El Escorial, for which he has to become director in 1576. Herrera, agenious of the Renaissance recently dedicated to architecture, would make a classical, universal and eternal style definitely triumph, that would erase from Spain such deeply established styles as Christian-Moorish and Plateresque.

In 1582 the Lonja of Seville was begun according to the designs of Herrera. They were carried out by one of his faithful men, Juan de Minjares, and finished by Alonso de Vandelvira. The outside is Herrera style: free, pure, sharp. The stone contrasts with the pointed, colored brick. The patio has the same grandeur as the one of the Evangelists in El Escorial.

Two centuries later the great King Carlos III gave this palace the most noble of destinies: that of being the Archive of the grandest enterprise ever undertaken by a nation: that of discovering, conquering, evangelizing, colonizing, humanizing and populating an empty and silent continent, from pole to pole and from sea to sea. The cases and shelves, carved by Blas Molner and Juan de Astorga, are made of wood from Cuba. These hold thirty-eight thousand papers and documents, including the most important Diary of Columbus and the Mapa Mundi of Juan de La Cosa —the narrative and graphic birth certificates of América— which contain the names of the conquerors of the sea, of the semi-gods of the epic poems, of the embassadors of Christ, of those who took, with them wheat, the horse, the wheel and the plough, of those who moved the University, Law, Dignity and Liberty, of those who gave their flesh, their blood and their word to fill an empty, silent continent with a dark smile and a sweet accent.

The outside of the Archive of the Indies, with the Cathedral in the background. →

ATESA

A room of the Archive of the Indies.

GARDENS AND MARÍA LUISA PARK

Visitors to Seville can enjoy the pleasantness of the city's public gardens. The cession of the Huerta del Retiro —that was inside the Alcázar— gave way to the birth of the Gardens of Catalina Ribera, which, being very bare at their creation in 1898, were preferred by sorrowful families, thereby receiving the name «Walk of those in mourning». In 1920 great reforms were made and the results were the gardens that we find today, with tall trees, walks, trellises, baskets of blowers, circular benches and the monuments dedicated to Christopher Columbus —designed by Talavera and made by Coullaut Valera— and to Catalina Ribera, a Doric entrance with a rustic flavor, niches with paintings that represent the noble woman and some of her most important foundations; at the foot of this monument, there is a XVI century fountain in marble, that was previously in the plaza del Pumarejo and in the Hospital de la Sangre.

Thanks to the donation of Alfonso XIII, in 1911, the gardens of Murillo were created and they appear with jazmine, trellises of roses, ivy and creepers, streets with center circles, marbles, tiles, inlays in the benches and backs, and palm trees, especially in the lovely section of Refinadores. These gardens have been cared for with greater attention each day, perhaps in compensation for the land they lost when the Ronda was widened.

The gardens of Cristina, of marked English or natural character, were the result of the urbanization on the back of the river that was initiated by the chief officer of justice Arjona in 1830; at the beginning of the century, the gardens were reduced in size to make way for bridges, and soon after, for the hotels for the Iberoamerican Exposition.

In 1893, the princess María Luisa Fernanda, duchess, widow Montpensier, gave Seville half of the gardens —where the romantic idyl Alfonso XII and Mercedes had walked— of her palace of San Telmo. «The Park of María Luisa» has two distinct periods; the first until 1929, the second from the Exposition to the present. The first witnesses the miracle of how the aristocratic foliage, under the direction of a French engineer, is subjected to norms such that the people of Seville, able to come and go peacefully, along its walks and paths, enjoy the trees, gardens and flowers on the banks of the Guadalquivir. We could talk of poplar, lotus, pecan, evergreen and palm trees, chestnuts from the Indies; of ponds, grottos, pergolas, benches, because when they thought that the head gardener was going to build a cold labyrinth of vegetation, like Versalles, he produced, instead, this warm, free and cozy marvel.

Monument to Columbus, in the Gardens of Murillo.

Monument to Gustavo Adolfo Bécquer, in the María Luisa Park.

Three views of the popular María Luisa Park. →

Aerial view of the City Hall and the Nueva Plaza.

Detail of one of the doors of the City Hall (XVI c.).

THE EXPOSITION; ALIVE

The second phase of the María Luisa Park begins when, as a result of the decree of the concession to Seville of the Iberoamerican Exposition, buildings spring up in the lap of the green of the Park for the pavillions. It is a critical moment, because one could think that the new constructions might erase the personality of the park or at least change its appearance drastically. Then the miracle: the buildings are in unvelievable accord with the landscape, or they have created a new landscape which is even more beautiful.

There is the Plaza de España, facing the river, with the park in between, perhaps the grandest and most graceful building of the XX century, entirely Spanish and Andalusian; it is deeply established on idea, materials and hand labor; tradition, plain brick, tiles and the love of craftsmen who have known their trade for over a thousand years. Once a colonel was told to place his regiment in the Plaza de España and he asked if they would all fit; it is large enough for an entire Army of men. Beneath the pointed towers, we find the covered galleries, the sections of the Spanish provinces with their symbols and their history in tiles. And enclosing the plaza, there is a pond.

The people of Seville did not want the Exposition to be of poor quality, of reeds and plaster that would be torn down the following day and so everything was made from noble materials destined to remain. If, during the last 15 years, the directors of Seville had correctly forseen the development of the world, Seville today would be a universal capital and would have had for years the title of «City of Conventions» that has just been given to Barcelona. Perhaps the saying «Seville in Spring» —the Spring of Holy Week and the Fair— could still be surpassed by «Come to Seville in Autumn». It is true that then there is no fragrance of the orange blossoms, but there is the smell of damp earth because the country is still very near and not beyond a never ending forest of asphalt; one can feel the land stretching after a shower; Seville, in Autumn, with the heat past, now centered in the fruit of the orange trees, with bright, clean air and the palms swaying in the breeze, is the ideal city for work, conversation, conferences and dialogue; for rest, a walk and an excursion.

The Great Casino of the Exposition and its annex the Theater Lope de Vega —large, lovely and elegant— could be converted into an authentic Convention Palace —offices, committee rooms, assembly halls, projection rooms, translating equipment, teletype, bars, restaurants, etc; in other words, the thousand and one details that must be improvised because Seville is never fraudulent, but these could be solved so that all the congresses, conventions, symposiums, days, weeks, meetings could accept our invitation to «Come to Seville in Autumn».

A view of the plaza de España. →

The Plaza de España offers a grand view.

Archaeological Museum. Treasure of «Carambolo» and a view of one of the rooms.

Archaeological Museum. Statue of the Emperor Trajano, from Itálica.

Archaeological Museum. Immense head of Augustus, from Itálica.

Hospital of Charity. Detail of the main altarpiece, by Pedro Roldán. →

A view of the plaza de Cuba.

Walls of the Macarena.

Gardens in the María Luisa Park.

The Plaza de la Virgen de los Reyes.

Jesus of the Great Power, by Juan de Mesa: «...the Divine seed from your blood / flows eternally like the river...».

Virgin of the Macarena (XVII c.).

Holy Week. The «Paso» of Our Lady of Anguish. →

THE PLAZA DE AMERICA AND THE ARCHAEOLOGICAL MUSEUM

One of the clearest, gayest and most noble plazas of which Spanish urbanism can boast was constructed on land from the María Luisa Park and the Huerta de Mariana. Here we find various architectural styles along with the noise of water, the grace of the flowers and the decorative curtain of the woods. The Plaza de América is bordered by the Pabellón Mudéjar, on the north, the Pabellón Real in flaming Gothic, on the east, and the Pabellón Renacimiento, in Plateresque, on the south.

The Pabellón Mudéjar is used for exhibits of all kinds of art. The Pabellón Real today houses the municipal urban offices. They were built and decorated by the most notable artists of the period, under the direction of don Aníbal González, forming a new, truly Golden Era in Seville.

In 1946, the Archaeological Museum of Seville was installed in the Pabellón Renacimiento. This should be a place of pilgrimage for the people of Seville and a visit not to missed by national and foreign tourists who pass through the city, as much because of the richness and interest of its contents as for the beauty of the setting itself. We Spaniards are what we are in virture of an inheritance of six thousand years. A contribution of one thousand years lives with us: we must look for what came before, in order to be familiar with it and to know ourselves.

The contents of the Museum is the work of a few patrons and interested parties; the first Marquis of Tarifa, Parafán de Ribera, Francisco de Bruna, Ivo de la Cortina, Demetrio de los Ríos, Gestoso, Gago, and a few others. These are not many considering the large area that is still waiting for the wise, methodical and loving pickaxe.

The rooms of the Museum are dedicated, in order, to prehistoric objects or historical ones before Rome, the first signs of the existence of man in the valley, who left his religious unrest in the dolmens of Matarrubilla and the Pastora; Iberian art with its high point between the III and I century before Christ; the Roman remains from the legal convents of Seville and Écija («hispalense» and «astigitano»); various pieces from Itálica; Greek statuary that reached Itálica when it was the second city of the Empire, and Roman statues with the masterpieces Aphrodites, Anadyomene, Atleta crowned, Diana and Mercury.

Since a short while ago, they have been exhibiting the Treasure of the Carambolo, along with which, in the María Luisa Park, next to the still warm testimony of the Iberian and Roman «Bética» (Andalusia), we find the archaeological evidence of an undecipherable legend: Tartessos.

Archaeological Museum. Sculpture of a man, from Alcalá del Río; and the heads of Alejandro, Galba and Octavia, from Itálica.

Archaeological Museum. Hermes and Aphrodites from Itálica.

THE UNIVERSITIES

Almost face to face, or more correctly, back to back, we find two Universities: the one that was originally Mareantes' and the one that since a few years ago is the Universidad Hispalense. The first has been called for hundreds of years, the Palace of San Telmo, and the second, until the other day, The Tobacco Factory.

The University of Mareantes, established by the business of Seville to form good captains for the art of navegation, took as long to build as a Gothic cathedral: from 1682 to 1796; if the plans were faithfully carried out, it was due to the fact that Leonardo de Figueroa was followed by his son Matías and later by his grandson Antonio Matías; the grand father and son did the entrance on the west side, making the entire building be classified as Baroque or «churrigueresco», when it is really Neoclassic; this Neoclassic is no longer cold precisely because of this addition. The Nautical school ended in 1847, and in 1849 —a short interval of Humanities— it became the palace of the small plots of the Montpensiers to sit on the throne of Isabel II. These efforts were compensated for, in a way, because a Spanish queen did come from that palace. The Princess who gave the Park, at her death, also gave the Palace to the Mitra, that converted it into the Mayor Seminary, which it still is today.

The Tobacco Factory was begun in 1728 and finished in 1770; the plans and the initial construction was by the Flemish architect Van der Berg, followed by Catalá and José Herrera, who finished it. The structure, including the moats, is perhaps the third or fourth largest civil building in Spain, and it has been said that around 1800 there were about twelve thousand people working there. The majority of workers were women, thousands and thousands of «Carmens», who, if not with knives in their garters, then certainly with carnations in their hair, lavored over the tobacco, until fifteen years ago.

Since then, the bricklayers and stonecutters have been working inside and out, to change an immense factory into a huge educational institution. They have been trying to give the new doors —one on each side, although the North one is still missing— the same grandeur and nobility that the original entrance had. This is in Neoclassic style with an allegory to tobacco, praise for the discoveror of its land, Columbus, and for the first European smoker, Hernán Cortés, in addition to other references to the character of the «militarized firm», with jurisdiction, court and jail in its powerful citadel, the guardian of the profits from the monopolized products.

Main entrance to the Palace of San Telmo, today the main Seminary. →

Aerial view and the entrance to the Tobacco Factory, today the University.

SEVILLE, GUADALQUIVIR...

And then there came the day when a choice had to be made between poetry and efficiency. Efficiency won.

The poetry consisted in continuing to sing to the Guadalquivir as it passed through Seville, as they had done since long, long ago. Because the «Betis» is perhaps the most highly praised river in the world, and there is a reason why. It has been confirmed that the oldest and most flowering Iberian civilization, the legendary Tartessos, was located on these banks, plains and hills, thereby proclaiming it the Treasure of the Carambolo and the unequalled pure gold ornament discovered in Mulva in the XI century before Christ. The oldest province in the Roman Empire, «Bética», that gave Rome emperors, poets, olives, seasonings and dancers, was established on the basis of the river. By way of the river, the escape of the Vandals and the invasion of the Moslems. By way of the river, the entrance of all the Hellenic culture, carried by the invaders from África and Alexandría in Asia and remade in Seville and Córdoba. By way of the river, the frustrated attempts of the Normans and the reconquesting calvacades of Fernando III.

In the Guadalquivir, the ships from the recently discovered lands of the New World. By way of the Guadalquivir, the departure of Magellan and Elcano who were going around the world. By way of the Guadalquivir, the transcendential deeds of arms that began the ruin of the «Grande Armee» of Napoleón. The Guadalquivir carries a lot of history with it which must be remembered. And much poetry. Don Juan Tenorio thought he was reciting a verse —Seville, Guadalquivir—, when he was really creating a tourist slogan.

But for efficiency's sake, so that Seville would not suffer from floods, the «new river bed» was made in 1928, taking the water from beneath the bridges and forming a sure, comfortable inner harbor, always with the same water level, regulated by locks; this magnificent inner harbor is 100 kilometers from the sea, to be improved by the Seville-Bonanza Canal.

Beyond Triana, we find the real, flowing river, and anyone can see that it is different from others; because it does not always flow toward the sea, but rather also inland when the tide rises. This river —although it seems vain to say so— is not just a river, but also an arm of the sea.

The bridge of Alfonso XIII or of Tablada.

«The afternoon is hanging / along the river». →

THE RIVER BANKS OF SEVILLE

It is fashionable these days to decorate offices with large photographic reproductions of old engravings of Seville, especially those that show the river banks of the Guadalquivir; the angle of the walls of the outlet of the Tagarete; the activity on the beaches and piers located beneath the Tower of Gold; the view of the Cathedral and the Giralda with the Arenal and the port in the foreground; the Bridge with boats that tied Triana to the Magdalena and the Merced at the back; the belfries and towers of the convents in the surrounding area, etc. It is possible that this new fashion will make the people of Seville become again interested in the river, as they did centuries ago when a holiday was proclaimed at the arrival of the ships from the Indies or when the entire city crowded together to watch Magellan's departure.

We have already said that in Seville there is not a river, but rather an inner harbor regulated by locks. Next to these, we find the racks and buildings of the Elcano Shipyards, the large installations of the fertilizer factory, the thermal center of Guadaira, the oil and mineral docks. Upstream, the Port of Seville, where numerous goods are imported and exported, the back of the Gardens of the Delicias, the María Luisa Park, the Gardens of San Telmo and of Cristina; and now we are at the Tower of Gold, a watch tower fortress and key to the Guadalquivir, since, with a chain attached to a strong, solid mass of mortar on the opposite bank, the port was closed. It was built by the Almohade Moors in 1220 or 1221 so that the river, the towers and the chains would serve as a heraldry to the village of Avilés; but Rui-Pérez took it in 1248, only twenty-eight years after its erection. This structure is of large stones, with a dodecagonal foundation and a second body with merlons and golden tiles. A wall connected it to the Tower of Silver —octagonal and today absorbed into the houses— which was connected to the Alcázar. The Hospital of Charity was built, in the XVII century, between the wall and the river.

The tragic soul of Andalusia is represented in the notable Baroque altarpiece by Pedro Roldán, the exceptional paintings by Murillo which are severe but which did not attain the ascetic fury that Miguel de Nañara wanted, and in the masterly, Baroque, realistic, unadorned, violent, impetuous and obsessional canvases by Valdés Leal which are nothing more than the graphic expression of the «Discussion of Truth», in clear opposition to so much «joy, light and color» of the tambourine.

The Tower of Gold, an Almohade construction, so called because of the its gold tiles.

Hospital of Charity. One of the canvases of the «Last Stage» by Juan de Valdés Leal.

BULLS IN LA MAESTRANZA

Whether the fans from other regions like it or not, the announcement that there are «Bulls in La Maestranza» can fear competition, only at a distance, from «Bulls in Ronda» and «Bulls in Puerto». The ring also plays a part. In the art of bull fighting there are the equivalents that can be noticed in any poster... «for Diego Puerta, from San Bernardo, Curro Romero, from Camas, Jumillano, from Albacete, and Curro Girón from Venezuela»: a neighborhood in Seville, a town in Andalusia, a province in the rest of Spain, a country in South America. The ring of La Maestranza in Seville must now be —after the enlargement of the one in Pamplona, inaugurated during the festivities of San Fermín in 1967— the third or fourth largest, but it is still and will continue to be the first in beauty.

Where else can the spectator, sitting in the shade on an April afternoon, take in, with a single glance, the golden earth, the mark of the protagonists, the color of the public in the sun and the Giralda emerging over the red rooftops amidst a crystal-clear atmosphere, pointing toward the blue sky? When thinking of the Maestranza, we remember the verses: «Unfolded capes in the afternoon — feet firm in the golden sand —silk and gold, blood and sun, the bull fighter— in a dream of deaths and swords thrusts».

In La Maestranza, the great step forward in the history of bull fighting, when José «—Joselito el Gallo — flower of the bull fighting race — the girls of Seville — cry for you in Spring—» and Juan —Juan Belmonte, the «monster», «the earthquake of Triana»— entered and took ground from the bulls. Joselito, who died in the ring of Talavera with his slippers on, has a mausoleum in the Cemetery of San Fernando, born of the inspiration of Mariano Benlliure, and a monument in his birthplace Gelves. Juan, who died in the pasture beside his own bulls in 1962, is now going to have his monument in the plaza del Altozano, at the entrance to Triana.

And both, face to face, heart to heart, will also be perpetuated in medallions, next to the sands of their glories, on the walls of this Real Plaza de la Maestranza de Caballería, which was begun in 1760 by Vicente San Martín, rebuilt in 1777 and finished in 1880 by Juan de Talavera. The entire construction is in simple classic style, with a stone interior, except for the brick arches on top of marble columns; the entrance has Tuscan and Doric columns; the inside door is Ionic and Corinthian; the royal box has a dome of stone worked in Greco-Roman style. It is a ring, in other words, where it is worthwhile to risk your life between the half moon of the horns.

The opening march in La Maestranza, the first bull ring in the world.

Provincial Museum of Fine Arts. Portrait of Jorge Manuel Theotocopuli, by El Greco. →

Provincial Museum of Fine Arts. The Virgin of the Caves,
by Zurbarán.

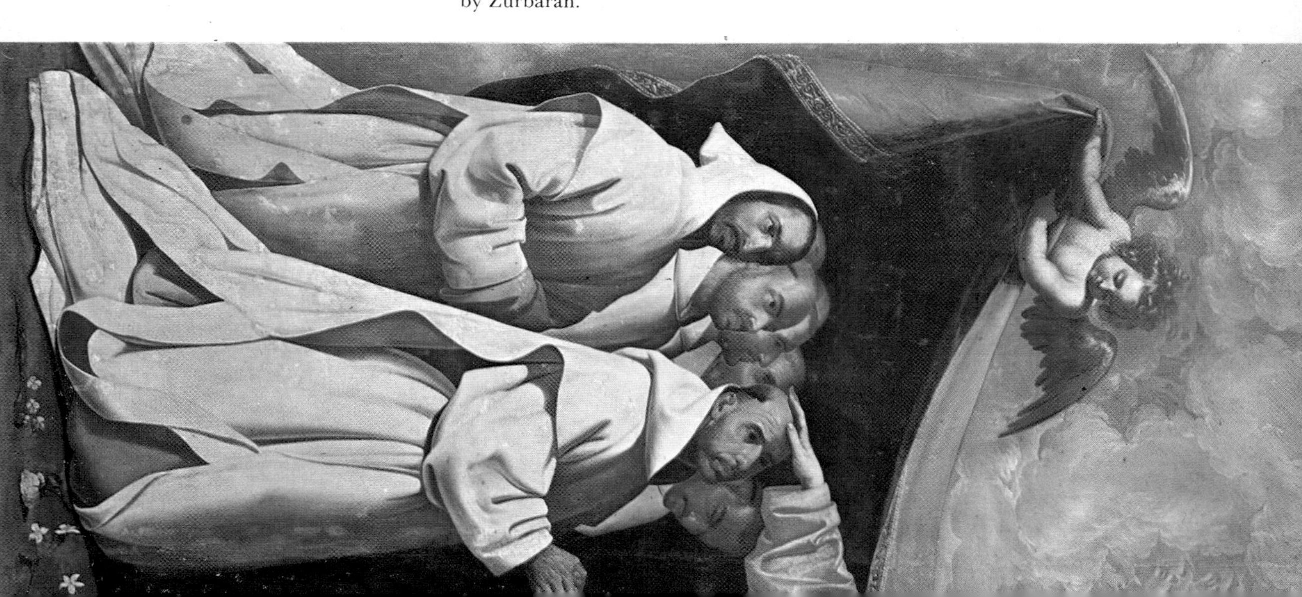

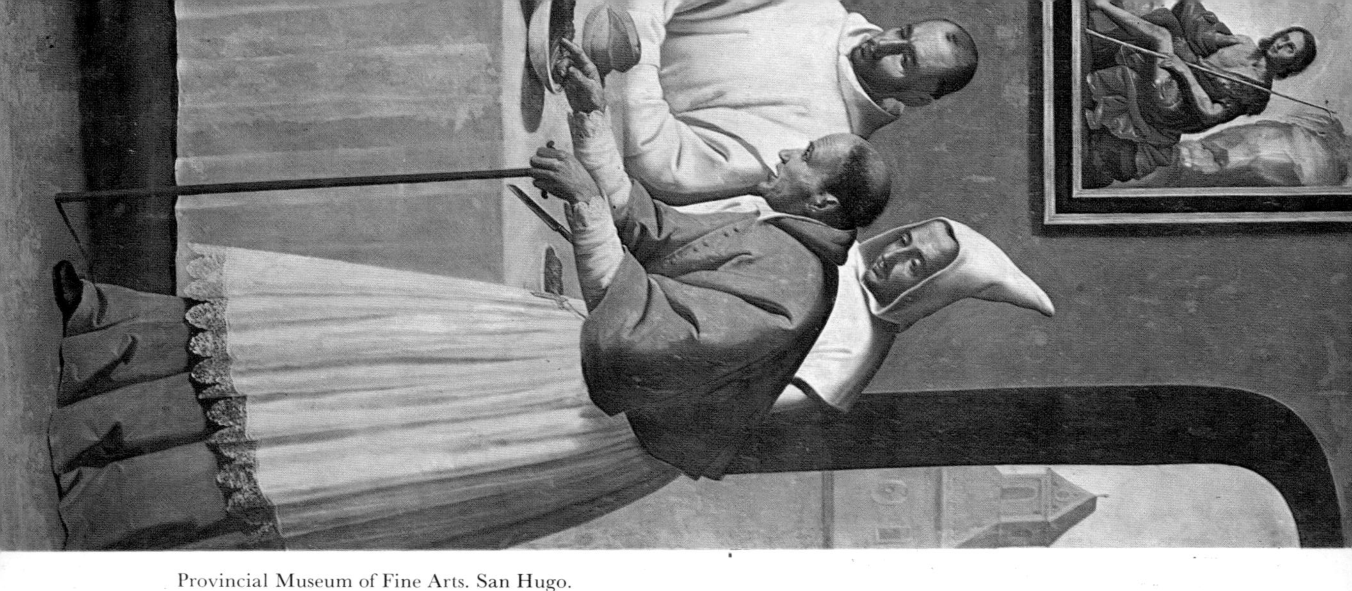

Provincial Museum of Fine Arts. San Hugo.
The Miracle of St. Voto, by Zurbarán.

Provincial Museum of Fine Arts. Sts. Justa and Rufina, by Murillo.

Provincial Museum of Fine Arts. Inmaculada by Murillo:
«Of celestial and Sevillana grace...».

THE MAGDALENA AND THE MUSEUM

When speaking of the Museum of Paintings, officially the Fine Arts Museum, let it suffice to say that it is the second picture gallery in Spain. In regard to the church of the Magdalena, we can affirm that it is a museum of religious sculpture from the Seville School, the most important of all religious imagery.

The works of art, mainly paintings, that were to comprise the future museum, came from the secularization of 1835; patient experts collected and catalogued all that the monks had abandoned. And all this treasure was placed in the old convent of the Merced, which had been built by Juan de Oviedo two centuries before. Even with modifications and additions, the exceptional content has a dignified, harmonious, grand and at the same time intimate countenance that makes us experience the paintings with a special emotion. The entrance is from the XVIII century, added later to give majesty to the frugal and gay exconvent. The level multicolored tiles of the socle of the majority of the rooms, are the original ones from the XVI and XVII centuries, also taken from many other convents falling to ruin.

Here we find the best collection of paintings by Murillo, twenty-four by Zurbarán and others by Valdés Leal, nineteen by Pacheco, fourteen by Herrera el Viejo, five by Roelas and many more, just to mention the classical ones.

The parish of the Magdalena, whose walls were falling down, came to rest in the convent of the Dominican Fathers of San Pablo, whose grand church, one of the notable ones from the XVIII century, was to fall to ruin. In the main altarpiece, we find the Magdalena, a prodigious sculpture by Felipe Malo de Molina. The union of two rich treasures will make the temple the most ornamental one in the city, and for this reason, we have called it a sculpture museum. We must mention:

«Virgin with the child», by Torrijiano; «Conception», by Martínez Montañés or Duke Cornejo; the «Virgin of the Presentation», by Juan de Astorga; «Christ of the Calvary», by Francisco de Ocampo; the «Altarpiece of the Ascent», by Juan de Mesa; the «Virgin of the Rosary», by Cristóbal Ramos; the Altarpiece of the Chapel of the Fifth Anguish, by Pedro Nieto; «Risen Christ» and «Child Jesus», by Jerónimo Hernández; the «Virgin of the Fevers», «St. Ann and the Virgin», «St. Rose» and the «Virgin of Protection», and others that religious piety has prevented from identifying their authors; on one hand, because it is considered irreverent to undress them, and, on the other, because of the colors, varnishes and retouching they have withstood during centuries.

In 1919 work was done in the chapel of the Fifth Anguish; on tearing down various flat ceilings, they discovered three Moorish knot domes; the center one is an architectural gem. That day the workers were the central figures in an oriental tale.

Provincial Museum of Fine Arts. Triptych-altarpiece representing the Virgin with the Child and the saints Miguel and Bartolomé.

Provincial Museum of Fine Arts. The Virgin of the Napkin, a lovely work by Murillo.

← Provincial Museum of Fine Arts. «The embarcation of St. Pedro Nolasco» and the «Temptation of St. Jerónimo» by Alonso Vázquez and Juan de Valdés Leal, respectively.

Provincial Museum of Fine Arts. St. Jerónimo, a sculpture in baked clay by Pedro Torrigiano (1525).

Provincial Museum of Fine Arts. The Deification of St. Tomás de Aquino, one of the masterpieces by Zurbarán (1631).

THE BRIDGES AND LOS REMEDIOS

The pontiffs of the Roman Empire did not build bridges from Córdoba to the sea, because the «Betis» played tricks, changing its course: from Itálica it would go to Miraflores or to Alameda de Hércules and experts say that even in the street Sierpes, there was a dock. The boatmen of the region existed until a short time ago —the bridge-boat of Coria still runs— and those of Seville were famous, as is indicated at the base of the Giralda where there are plaques dedicated to Lucio Castricio and Sexto Julio. In order to communicate with Triana, they had a boat run until, in 1852, the Bridge of Isabel II was inaugurated. This is a copy of the Carrousel of the Seine, whose arches and cast iron astragals have cristalized in such a way that, in 1962, they had to repave it on top of reinforced concrete and prohibit heavy vehicles from using it. The bridge of the railway line to Huelva dates back to 1880.

The Exposition was the cause of great engineering feats: canal and lift bridge of Alfonso XIII; «New river bed» running behind Triana, converting it into an island, and the bridge of San Telmo, that was of the lift type until 1965 when it was widened and made stationary for the heavy traffic toward the new city, that is the neighborhood or sector Los Remedios, and toward Triana, that has changed so much in appearance. In 1968, they will inaugurate the new Generalísimo bridge, between San Telmo and Alfonso XIII, because Los Remedios will have more than 200,000 inhabitants and there are plans to place the Fair at its back.

It is said that Los Remedios is used as an example in the Architectural Schools of the world of how a new urbanization Should Not Be. They have taken land from the river and have given it, lengthwise, to the Real Círculo de Labradores, for its wonderful sports installations; to the new Tobacco Factory, that has already moved its processional «pasos» or floats to a new chapel; to the stone paved bridge Generalísimo, and to the Nautical Club, the promoter of victorious rowers. The streets, designed for one family dwellings, have been swallowed up in skyscrapers, and those that could reach the river are cut off at Asunción, as are other intersecting streets that shut out the view from the Hill of the Sacred Hearts; and now when the bridge is finished, the large avenue Virgen de Luján, which will double in size, will end before coming out into the highway that by-passes the city.

The bridge of Triana

The Plaza de Cuba.

The Patio of the Círculo de Labradores

TRIANA

The XIII century, the century of the great pure Gothic cathedrals of León, Burgos and Toledo, witnessed the arrival of Christians in Seville and when it seemed logical that the Castillian and northern masters would begin to build in ogival style, they joined hands with the Arab and Mauritanian masters —from Seville—, limiting themselves to change the mosques into churches, by inverting the axes. Without realizing it, they created or recreated the Christian-Moorish style, which, in addition, would fill the entire XIV century.

In 1280, Alfonso X ordered the erection of a temple on a new foundation on the other bank, and, in this way, we can point out the church of Santa Ana as the only example of Romanic-ogival style. It was finished in the XIV century and repaired, without much luck, in later centuries. The sculptures of Santa Ana and the Virgin are XIII century Romanic, while all the rest, altarpieces and paintings, is from the first half of the XVI century, signed by the Flemish artists Pedro de Campaña and Francisco Fruted and, among the Spaniards, Alejo Fernández Alemán.

Triana was the maritime bank of Seville; the men were the boatmen, the pontoniers, the sailors who went with Columbus and Magellan and with the fleets to the Indies, the runners of the codfish boats, the sanders, the voluntary sailors of the Crusade, the harbor workers and the Esperanza, which, when passing the bridge, is lighted by war ships at dawn on Good Friday.

Triana, «a garden of flowers at every window», as a welcome to those who reached home after long overseas voyages or short runs between Villanueva with coal and Bonanza with salt.

So much water from the «Betis» made Triana become located on —and surrounded by— a large, deep blanket of virgin, ductile clay, unending soft ground that was to play a part in the other side of its personality: ceramics. Tall chimneys, walls of immense enclosures, Moorish ovens, Moorish roof tiles, tiles like those of the Alcázar, like those of the XVI and XVII centuries, that are exported —increasingly less and less— to Morocco and América so that they can continue to build in the oriental or colonial style.

Triana has been the name adopted by many bull fighters, singers and dancers, at times by entire dynasties of gypsy artists.

The hard wet winters since 59 have levelled the colorful houses; the price of land and the legislation in regard to bothersome industries, abolished the ceramic factories, the means of transportation erased the personality, and today Triana, without the geraniums on its balconies, without chimneys smelling of grape refuse fuel and without gypsies, is just another neighborhood in a modern city.

Chapel of the Patrocinio. Christ of the Expiration, popularly called «El Cachorro», a carving by Francisco Antonio Gijón (1682). →

THE OTHER RIVER

At the very foot of the dam of Alcalá, where the Atlantic tides end, the Guadalquivir turns south; it carries very little water to Ribera de Huelva, being held in the dam of the Minilla or stopped for its use in Lagos del Serrano; then, it finds itself with the recently opened stream Tamarguillo and it enters Seville by way of San Jerónimo, leaving to the left, the ruins of one of the two large XV century monasteries.

The other monastery was the Cartuja or Santa María de las Cuevas, on the right, with a strange appearance in which the conventual outlines are mixed with kilns, since it was sold in 1838 and its buildings were notably changed for the installation of the famous «La Cartuja» ceramics. Here one can buy pottery as well as contemplate the Christian-Moorish styled little cloister and Capítulo chapel or the ogival arches at the entrance, with a second section that was added in the XVI century, and the naves of the church.

Christopher Columbus' remains rested in the chapel of Santa Ana between 1507 and 1537. And when it was disassembled, the magnificent tombs of the Riberas were moved to the old University. The inscriptions on the tombs give the history of Andalusia, of those who were Governors, Admirals and a number of titles won with blood, since «They gave their lives in the Moorish wars». There are beautiful marbles by Aprile Pedro and Gaspar de la Scala, Baldasari, Bernardine. In October of 1964, they discovered the tomb of Perafán de Ribera which was later moved beside those of his lineage, and recently, the city of Tarifa requested the tomb of the first Marquis, don Fadrique Enríquez de Ribera.

Almost in front, on the river bank of Seville, we find the Tower of Don Fadrique, the only Gothic civil monument from the XIII century, erected by the brother of Alfonso X. It has a square foundation, built with large stones and brick, and with merlons on the third dome.

The embankment, the bridges, for the train and the highway to Huelva, the sand docks, the installations of prefabricated concrete, the small tile works, the orange orchards and the river goes toward San Juan, toward Gelves, and through Coria —now united with the other branch— flows into the marsh, where the bulls are pushed out by the enslaving advance of rice beds.

 Tomb of D. Pedro Enríquez, in the church of the old University. →

← «The marsh, that the bulls abandon in the face of the forceful advance of the rice beds».

HIC IACET FRANCISCVS DVARTEVS VIR CLA
RISSIMVS MILITARIVM COMEATVVM C V C
AVG PRA MAX QVI MVLTIS PROFVIT E NE
MINI NOCVIT ET D CATHERINA DE MOER
CONIVX SVA OBIIT VIII OCTO MDLIIII

Cathedral. Patio of the Oranges, that was the Main Mosque (XII c.).

House of Pilatos. Main patio. →

From the tomb of Francisco Duarte de Mendioca and his wife in the church of the old University.

STILL ORIENTAL

Investigators want the archaeological remains of Seville, the capital, to start, in ancient times, with the Giralda. Nothing remains from Rome, that surrounds us with the Necropolis in Carmona and the Amphitheater in Itálica. The original walls and monoliths in the open in the street Marmoles —visible from the same ground level of the city two thousand years ago—, undoubtedly the location of a great temple, were placed in the Alameda de Hércules, in the XVI century. From Visigothic Seville, we only have the capitals used in the Alcázar, Cathedral, the Patio of Oranges and private homes, in addition to the bowl of the fountain of the Patio —that originally had a dome— and the stele in front of the prison of San Hermenegildo.

Is it possible that nothing remains of the Arab Ixvilia, in power from the VIII century and at its peaks at the end of the IX and during all of the X, a part of the caliphate or independent from the Abbasita Moors? Ixvilia did not see the cruel civil wars that took place in Córdoba, nor is it supposed that the Almoravid fury in control for 55 years completely destroyed it. No matter what fanatics they were, some mosques would remain, with their minarets intact and the Almohades would put the mark of gaiety over them, and then, in the XIV century, they would be Christianized when the mosques were converted into churches.

Here we find the lovely and completely unique, in Europe, minarets of Santa Catalina, San Marcos, Santa Marina —the three along the same path from the downtown area to La Macarena— and Omnium Sanctorum. The three last churches suffered from a fire in July of 1936 and the only thing saved from the insides was the Virgin of All the Saints, by Roque Balduque. The fact that Santa Catalina has been declared a «National Monument» is an indication that it is an architectural jewel, which, in addition, contains very notable altarpieces and paintings.

The four minarets were more or less restored at the end of the last century or the beginning of the present one. The beautiful square towers, of thick brick, at one time with large stones at the lower corners, decorated with ogivas and «axaracas», once topped by merlons, small cupolas or spheres, were completed with the addition of belfries in San Marcos (XVI century) and Omnium Sactorum (XVII century), while in the other two, the bells were placed in the Moslem ogivas.

And there is also something purely oriental in the Patio of the Oranges.

Christian-Moorish tower of the church of San Marcos. →

NTIL E INDUSTRIAL
CINE
LLORENS
DEPORTE
LA CATALANA
NACIONAL
SEGUROS GENERALES
SEGUROS GENERALES
SALVAJE
MARLON BRANDO
caja de ahorros

CONVENTS

The Andalusian convents, especially those of Seville, have a special literature, perhaps because the Plateresque silhouette of their belfries, the familiar air of their music, the presence of flowers and the shining lime of their walls, make us think that behind the gates, the rough contemplative life is not quite so strict. The television report on the convent of Santa Paula is circling the world, because it has been able to capture the beauty and grandeur —inside and out— of the houses dedicated to God, the first Christian foundations in the land of Holy Mary, since San Clemente and Santa Clara, were of the Order of San Fernando, although they were later completely redone.

The music of Santa Clara —more monumental— and of Santa Paula —even more poetic—, as well as the Neoclassic atrium with portico of San Clemente, create a gay mystic feeling. All the churches of these monasteries have a single nave, but the entrances of Santa Paula —Gothic, Christian-Moorish and Renaissance all at the same time, with ceramic by Pisano and medallions by Pedro Millán—; of Santa Isabel —the most delicate of all of Alfonso de Vandelvira's work, fortunately visible since 1965—; of Santa Clara —in the shelter of the elegant portico by Diego de Quesada, almost in the shade of the Tower of Don Fadrique—; of the Madre de Dios —stone work by Juan de Oviedo for the Virgen del Rosario—; all have their own special characteristics.

The ceilings are Christian-Moorish in style, and as outstanding, we must point out the marvelous one in Madre de Dios, the Mozarabic golden pineapples in San Clemente, the exactness of the ones in Santa Paula. In the altarpieces of the convents —all from the XVII century, the great century in religious imagery— we find master works by artists with the chisel: Martínez Montañés did the five altarpieces of Santa Clara, the figures of the Baptist and the Evangelist in between the two that Alonso Cano did for Santa Paula, the «Last Judgement» in Santa Isabel whose center is the moving «Christ of Mercy», by Juan de Mesa, The Baptist in Santa María del Socorro and the one of the St. Johns in San Leandro, with the tremendous decapitated head of the Baptist.

The main altarpiece of Santa Isabel is by Juan de Mesa. The one in San Clemente is a maximum work of art by Felipe de Ribas, from Córdoba, who also worked on those in Santa Paula. The main altarpiece of Santa Isabel and those of the Calvario are by the great master Jerónimo Hernández and the one of the Rosary in the Madre de Dios, in imposing Baroque style, is by Francisco Barahona. Francisco Ocampo, the creator of the lost altarpiece of Santa Paula, is the author of the Epistle in San Clemente, in collaboration with Gaspar Núñez Delgado.

And in all the convents, peace.

← The popular street Sierpes.

Temple of la Madre de Dios. Christian-Moorish ceiling in the Main Chapel (XVI c.).

← Convent of Santa Paula. Detail of the entrance of the church and the tomb of León Enríquez (XVI c.).

«SEVILLANO» PALACES

We have written «Sevillano» several times in referring to an autochtonous architectural style that can be seen if one walks a bit around the city before it is completely renovated. They assimilated the Moslem forms that were topped with Gothic to give the Christian-Moorish style, and the arrival of the Plateresque produced a new combination —not a mixture, but rather a combination, like in chemistry— that «went well with the climate and topography, the poetical fantasy and the sensuality of the popular spirit», forming the «Sevillano» style. «Influenced by the Italian Renaissance, the craftsmen of Seville left unmistakable examples of their great skill, combining the Plateresque fantasies and their ornate pilgrims with ornamental plasterwork and Mohammedan bow shapes and with the foliage, traceries and flaming lines of Gothic or Christian art».

The style began at the end of the XV century, reached its high point in the XVI and XVII centuries and was revived at the beginning of the XX and continued with the Exposition, transcending to the urbanizations immediately following —La Palmera, Porvenir, Nervión, Barrio de Santa Cruz—, it was the common style for palaces and private homes, although what remains from the great centuries are the first because of the nobility of their materials, and they too are falling under the pickaxe.

The House of the Dueñas, finished in the XVI century and improved in the XVII. Plateresque patio, high ogival gallery and Christian-Moorish ornate plasterwork. Plateresque arches, flowery ogival chapel with tiles with metalic highlights. Christian-Moorish ceilings.

House of Pilatos, from the same period; the Marquis of Tarifa brought all kinds of marble from Italy for the house. It has a Genoa entrance and in the Plateresque and Christian-Moorish Patio we find the best tile work in Spain and statues collected by Perafán de Ribera. All the ceilings are of wood with elaborate carving.

House of the Pinelos, the old residence of clergy and boarding house until 1965; today it is the property of the City Hall as a result of its donation by the Corte Inglés, perhaps to make up for the tearing down of the palaces of Sánchez-Dalp (from the XX century) and of the Guzmanes (from the XVI century) in the plaza del Duque, which, in twenty years, has lost three of its four sides. Parlade received inspiration in the patio of Pinelo for the palace of the Puerta de Jerez, today the Palace of Guardiola.

The House of the Countess of Lebrija houses an authentic museum of Roman Bética. The Palace of the Marquis of Aracena became, twenty years ago, the offices of the C.S.E. and the Palace of the Counts of Gelves —with patios and tile inlays from the XVI century—, until now the Hotel Madrid, has placed its «neck» beneath the pickaxe to turn over its «soul» —the lot— to Galerías Preciados.

In 1967, a lot of noise was made over the «death» of four palaces, along with the one of the Levies. Will we need more tears? There are still some palaces left.

Palace of the Dueñas: «my childhood is filled with memories of a patio in Seville...».

House of Pilatos. Detail of the panelling in the Salon del Pretorio.

House of Pilatos. Door of the chapel.

INTERIOR GARDENS

One of the first curious tourists that saw Seville from a plane, said: «Seville is an unending interior garden». Then, in 1935, it was only what we continue to call the old crown of the city. A crown bordered by the river and by the Rondas with their gates: Córdoba, Osario, Carmona, Carne, Jerez, Triana and Real, today nothing more than names, but it is a good idea to preserve them so that man will feel inscribed in history and in geography.

The country made into farm land, entered the city. In front of the Gate of Córdoba, the Convent of Capuchino Fathers, on the very path that the herdsmen used for their sheep and goats. At the back, the small farms where the few cattle grazed and, next to them, the gardens where pretty girls tended their flower gardens. The Quinteros have made reference to the beauty of the girls and their flowers.

The churches, convents, and palaces had teir interior gardens but, in addition, each house was in itself a garden, big or small, with real land or with earth filling the flower pots, in garden patios where the palm and the miniture orange trees grew amidst hydrangeas, «pilistras», ferns, asparagus and cactus plants, and the permanent blooming geraniums and carnations with «gitanillos», jazmine, begonias, colius in the unbelievable aroma of the lady of the night. Even inside the modest home which we call «un corral», the large patio was a well cared for garden, until «profit» reduced the size to make way for the «chinchanes» of transitory industries.

There were three factors that determined the special appearance of a house in Seville: the excess sun and light, tradition and the social structure. Each family was a complete world that lived inward, into itself, and the burning sun entered, not through the windows and balconies but rather already screened by the rooftops that outlined the sky, by the colored sky-lights and in the heat of summer, by the awning or «vela» that shaded the patio, cooled by the bubbling fountain.

When the tourist passes through Seville, he timidly looks into these patios filled with plants and flowers where the sound of running water can be heard. He would like the doors to open, one by one, of the houses on Abades, San Vicente, Moratín and so many other streets; the houses are not monuments and have not been declared of national interest, but they are emotionally moving because it is here that we find the authentic way of life of a people, according to its geography and tradition.

A geography and tradition that have been fighting such phenomena as «service», «conservation», «comfort», «price of Land» and that are losing with valor and bravery.

← Artistic entrance to a typical house in Seville.

The patios of Seville are cozy, shaded and beautiful.

The flower filled alley of Water.

A SMALL CATALOGUE

Twenty-two centuries, lived intensely, leaving a deep impression in art, history and poetry, do not fit into thirty pages. If two or three centuries remained mute for posterity, there are seven that are worth twenty-one.

We should say something about those mosques converted into Christian-Moorish churches in the XIII and XIV centuries, that were destroyed by earthquakes, fires, inclemencies and restorations, that can hardly be recognized for what they were, except for an occasional original remains, the common factor of the three naves —San Lorenzo has two more that were added in the XVII century— and the Christian-Moorish ceilings. The oldest mural paintings in Seville have been preserved on one of the original walls of San Lorenzo and on another respected during the total demolition of San Ildefonso: the Virgin of Rocamador and the Virgin of the Coral, both from the XIV century with clear Italian influences.

Belonging to this group we have: San Gil, whose presbyterial socle is a tile inlay from the year 1300; San Juan de la Palma, with the Virgin of Bitterness, by la Roldana; and the San Juan from Hita del Castillo; San Vicente, with altarpieces by Cristóbal Guadix and sculptures by Andrés de Ocampo and Felipe de Ribas; San Isidoro shows a tower-façade and its altarpiece is a canvas by Roelas in the marvelous frame done by Felipe del Castillo; San Lorenzo, whose tower is from the XV century, and in the altarpiece by Barahona we find the Christ of Protection by Francisco de Ribas, and the Virgin of Granada, by Roque Balduque; San Andrés, that shows separately the Gothic and Christian-Moorish styles on the outside and the altarpieces by Alonso Cano and Andrés del Castillo; San Esteban, with a XV century entrance and four canvases by Zurbarán in the main altarpiece by Luis de Figueroa; San Pedro, totally redone in the XVII century, with an altarpiece by Felipe de Ribas.

San Martín, from the XV century, with an altarpiece by Ocampo and paintings by Gerólamo Corrente Corregio, and the very interesting chapel of the old Seminary, have only one nave. The chapel of San José is entirely Baroque, dating from the XVII century, like the church of the Terceros that is in exotic Baroque, possibly Portuguese-colonial style.

El Salvador is a grand structure that was begun in the XVII century on the destroyed fountation of the old largest mosque —which can be detected in traces in the patio of oranges— and finished in the XVIII century by Leonardo de Figueroa. The altarpieces by Cayetano Acosta and José Maestre are immense. In the altarpiece of the Epistle we find the Christ of Love, by Juan de Mesa, and in the chapel of the Sagrario, the Jesus of Passion, by Martínez Montañés, both master works in the art of imagery.

From the XVIII century we have the Baroque temple of San Luis and the Neoclassic ones of San Ildefonso —that preserved the images done by Felipe de Ribas— Santiago and San Bernardo, that are also decorated in Baroque style —Barahona, Ocampo and Balduque— which was inherited from earlier temples.

Church of El Salvador. Christ of Love, by Juan de Mesa and Jesus of Passion, by Juan Martínez Montañés. →

Church of San Vicente. The Descent, by Andrés de Ocampo.

ne women of Seville during the April Fair.

A view of the April Fair.

HOLY WEEK

A Great Week and different all over Spain. «Holy Week in Seville is baptized paganism» —an idea that is valid for all the Holy Weeks in Andalusia—, where the people sing «saetas» with the rhythm of «marinetes» as the images pass in procession. Holy Week is lived and felt because the men belong to a «Cofradía» and because the people go into the streets to see, hear and pray.

It is an unending spectacle; year after year and always different; it is not the same to sit along the official route as to attend the departure of the «pasos» or floats in that parade of power, agility and sacrifice of the porters, so that the poles do not rub against the stones of the portico; or to contemplate the «pasos» at the turn into a typical small street, crossing over a bridge, being reflected in the water, passing beneath an arch, with a background of windows and iron bars, gardens, palm trees, walls, or when a Virgin sways at her arrival at the temple. Year after year and it always seems like the first time.

The air is filled with the smell of Spring, incense, wax, orange blossoms, and from Palm Sunday to Holy Saturday, fifty-two «Cofradías» do penance at the Cathedral —the oldest are from the XVI century and the newest from 1955 and 1956— with 100 floats, 43 of which are Virgins with canopies, two without camopies, 31 mystery «pasos», 15 crucifixes and 9 Nazarenes.

The oldest documented images in this procession are: The Christ of Burgos, by Juan Bautista Vázquez in 1573, and the Christ of the Expiration in the chapel of the Museum, done in a special substance from an Aztec secret by Marcos Cabrera in 1575. In 1620 the marvelous Juan de Mena signed the crucified Christ of the Students, the Nazarene Jesus of the Great Power and the Virgin of the Victory from the Tobacco factory. The Jesus of Passion, by Martínez Montañés, is on a float with 200 kilograms of filigree silver. The Crucified of the Little Black Ones is by Ocampo, done in 1622. «El Cachorro», molded in paste in the XVII by Ruiz de Gijón, is extremely weakened. The Macarena is attributed to la Roldana, because it is not possible that such delicate work was done by the hands of a man. The modern sculptures, by Castillo Lastrucci and Fernández Andrés, are the main ones in the line of the great school.

And the eternal Spring in the eternal Holy Week of Seville.

— Santiponce. Monastery of San Isidoro del Campo. The St. Jerónimo of the main altarpiece, by Martínez Montañés.

La Macarena: «On an altar of silver, lighted by a thousand flames».

← Holy Week: «In the peaceful night the trumpets sound...».

THE APRIL FAIR

You already know the history: Doña Isabel II in 1847 gave Seville the privilege of celebrating a live stock Fair, held annually, beginning on April 18, and the families of the province, full of imagination, move to the fair grounds to live for a few days, as if they were going camping, with such comforts as a nice canvas «caseta», reed furniture and cornucopias and pictures to give it atmosphere; behind, the kitchen, a good stock of wine to invite friends and strangers, who are always foreigners to Seville that cannot be treated as such. And at once we begin to hear the guitar, the clapping and the rhymic beating of feet.

With time, the Prado de San Sebastián was organized so that the Fair was the great joy, the great holiday of all the people from the capital and province, who share it with the foreigners; next to the individual «casetas», they built those of institutions, cities and towns, organizations, businessmen... Always, the black eyes, flamenca dresses, carnations in the lapels, and arms moving to that rhythm that is beyond description. Men come from the country, the mountains or the marshlands to decorate the backs of their sorrels or Carthusian or Anglo-Andalusian dappels with a pretty blond or brunette.

And all this in April, in the heigth of Spring, with the air heavy with the aroma of the orange blossoms, the sky crystalclear blue or filled with stars, and the people completely happy because the fair is there. They are happy because they become light-headed with the gaiety that surrounds them, with the musical background of clapping hands, while watching the riders pass, or drinking a glass of «manzanilla» wine, or eating with the family in the «caseta» of an organization, or observing the merry procession of horse-drawn carts in the direction of La Maestranza. All of Seville, by means of the radio stations, is filled with «sevillanas» so that there is no doubt that the Fair is there, waiting for us.

After one hundred and twenty years in the Prado, the April Fair, in a growth crisis, moves to Los Remedios. It will again spring forth with all its force, and it will appear to happen spontaneously because the expression later applied to so many places and so many festivities was invented for Seville: «it is an extravagance of merriment, light and color». And that is what it really is because night and day are confused between the sun and the lanterns, between the fun and the «faralaes».

← Four views of Holy Week in Seville.

A rider at the Fair. →

Five views of the very popular April Fair. →

AMISTAD

A CALL TO INDUSTRY

Although not a customary topic for guide books, there is no doubt that a great part of the tourists of today are as interested in becoming familiar with the present life and way of life as they are in imagining the past when they enter an oriental garden or a Gothic cloister. Also of interest to the tourists are the large factories, the specif industries of a region or the workshops that show a traditional, singular and different way of working with various materials. The tourist has the right and the obligation to become familiar with the industries of Seville, in those aspects that are unequalled in many of the cities of Spain; and to find something more than archaeology.

In the art of crafts, they usually show how the hands of angels make a veil or a «mantilla» from silk lace, or how the soul of the embroiderer of fine gold goes into the cloaks of Virgins or into the capes of bull fighters. The ceramic industry also has its habitual visitors since Spain was the cradle of this craft; the metal highlights were an invention of Andalusia and Lucca della Robbia copied the people of Triana in the technique of glazing pottery. Some tourists even reach the workshops of the gold and silver workers, to see and buy marvelous «platerescos».

We must open up the great industries, those that, up until now, have been visited exclusively by professional tourism. Here, for example, we must mention:

Olive factories, where we are amazed at the dry, exactness of the person who removes the pit, at the agility of the fingers of the one who stuffs them with a piece of red pimento, at the marvelous eye of the selector, who separates the bad, rain or hail marked fruit from the good.

In «Hytasa», that takes in the whole textile industry, the visitor can see how a flower is changed into a sheet, raw wool into a piece of suit material, a bud of course silk into a feminine froufrou.

«CASA», that in Seville manufactures the only jet plane invented in Spain, the «Azor». «Elcano Shipyards» with thousands of men, measuring, cutting, whelding, riveting, soldering in the noble trade of building a boat so that a cargo ship, a fishing boat, or a refrigerated fruit boat can slip from the racks with the final emotion of the meeting of the water and the hull of the ship.

The unbelievably automated bottling plants whose malt processing was considered, at least six years ago, the first in Europe, belong to Coca-Cola, Pepsi-Cola, Estrella del Sur and the Cruz del Campo.

At last, Seville can exhibit its treasure of work, productivity and organization with the same pride that it shows off the treasure of the Cathedral.

← «The rustling of the skirt / of your dress».

A woman embroidering in fine gold.

The crafts of Seville: Castanets and a fan.

HERE NEARBY

Here nearby, 30 kilometers away along the highway to Madrid, at the entrance to Carmona, we have Rome in its City of the Dead, one of the most notable of this type in all of the large Empire. The Necropolis was discovered during some grading work in 1869 and since then non-experts and professional men have been bringing the burial ground into the light, and there is still a lot to be uncovered. From the inscriptions found, it was used from the first century before Christ until the end of the IV, supposing that the little evolution of the types of tombs there over such a long period of time is a result of the impact of Christianity around the II century which limited the use of the Necrópolis to a few families who still were followers of paganism.

The tombs vary from the simplest type —a hole covered with tiles or flagstones— to the great mansion that gives the impression that the dead are still alive. There are one, two, three or more chambered tombs, the most interesting being the one of the Elefante and the one of the Servilia. Just to give us an idea, we can mention the fact that this last one was supposedly excavated in the soft rock of the hill, measuring 6,000 cubic meters; it is really a subterranean palace.

Here, seven kilometers along the road to Lusitania, we have Rome living in the ruins of Itálica: a city once opulent and wealthy became completely ignored, perhaps as a result of the action of unchained natural agents and the devastation of the men. The Hispanic-Roman rocks of Itálica were the source of limestone or large rocks for the houses in the Aljarafe or in Seville, flagstones for the roads, ornamentation of fortresses, palaces and churches; its statues and reliefs were stolen and destroyed. But there still remain street beds, sidewalks, entire stories of houses with their mosaic floors, the sewerage system, in other words, the perfect urbanization. At one side, we find the large Amphitheater whose size gives us an idea of the importance of the Itálica that Rodrigo de Caro wrote about in the XVI century.

Guzmán el Bueno erected the Monastery of San Isidoro del Campo with rocks from Itálica. The mortal remains of the immortal hero of Tarifa are laid to rest in the church which has one nave that he built and another that was attached shortly after by the son, Juan Pérez de Guzmán; both are connected by a large arch and form a single transept. We must stop to admire the ogival Christian-Moorish entrance, from the XV century, the Patio of the Dead, from the XIV, the Patio of the Evangelists, with paintings from the XV, both two stories high with galleries, and the beautiful altarpiece by Martínez Montañés.

Itálica. Ruins of the amphitheater. →

Carmona. A burial room in the Roman necropolis.

Itálica. A gallery in the amphitheater.

Santiponce. Monastery of San Isidoro del Campo.
Detail of the main altarpiece, by Martínez Montañés.

INFORMACION PRACTICA SEVILLA

INFORMATION PRATIQUE SEVILLE

PRACTICAL INFORMATION SEVILLE

PRAKTISCHE INFORMATION SEVILLA

La mayor parte de estos datos han sido facilitados por la Delegación Provincial de Información y Turismo de Sevilla.
Información puesta al día el 15-12-1969

La plupart des données ont été fournies par la Délégation Provinciale d'Information et Tourisme de Séville. Information mise a jour le 15-12-1969

The major part of this information has been facilitated by the Provincial Delegation of Information and Tourism of Seville. Information compiled. Dec. 15-1969

Der grösste Teil dieser Daten wurde uns von der Delegación Provincial de Información y Turismo von Sevilla zur Verfügung gestellt Die Angaben entsprechen dem 15-12-1969

CONJUNTO MONUMENTAL

LA CATEDRAL. Sobre el emplazamiento de la Mezquita Mayor de los almohades, de la que subsisten el Patio de Abluciones, la Puerta del Perdón y la famosa Giralda, se construyó la Catedral en el siglo XV, que por sus dimensiones, es la mayor de España y la tercera del orbe cristiano, siendo una interesante muestra del arte gótico. Su retablo es el mayor de toda la cristiandad. Rico tesoro y numerosas obras de arte por toda la Catedral: pinturas de Murillo, Goya, Pedro de Campaña, Luis de Vargas; esculturas de Martínez Montañés, Lorenzo Mercadante de Bretaña y otros.
Horas de visita:
Verano, de 10,30 a 12,30 y de 16 a 18,30.
Invierno, de 10,30 a 12,30 y de 15 a 17,30.
Precio de entrada: 20 pesetas.
La Giralda, alminar de la antigua mezquita, es de arte almohade (siglo XII), con el cuerpo de campanas del Renacimiento. Igual horario.
Precio de entrada: 5 pesetas.

REALES ALCAZARES. Palacio mudéjar, del siglo XIV, construido por Pedro I de Castilla sobre los antiguos palacios musulmanes, de los que subsiste el Patio del Yeso. Preciosos los Patios de las Doncellas y de las Muñecas y el Salón de Embajadores. Edificaciones posteriores de los siglos XV al XVIII. Maravillosos jardines, de varios estilos.
Horas de visita:
Verano, de 9 a 12,45 y de 16 a 18,45.
Invierno, de 9 a 12,45 y de 15 a 17.
Cerrado: 1 de enero, 25 de diciembre, Viernes Santo y Corpus Christi. Exposición permanente del Patrimonio Nacional. Festivos y domingos, sólo por las mañanas.
Precio de Entrada: 30 pesetas.

BARRIO DE SANTA CRUZ. Antigua judería, es el barrio típico de Sevilla, siendo de especial belleza el Callejón del Agua y la calle de la Pimienta y las plazas de Santa Marta, Doña Elvira y de Santa Cruz, con la Cruz de Cerrajería, verdadero encaje de hierro forjado del siglo XVII.

HOSPICIO DE LOS VENERABLES SACERDOTES Y MUSEO DE SEMANA SANTA. En pleno barrio de Santa Cruz. La iglesia es de estilo barroco y conserva notables obras de arte. Patio bellísimo. El Museo reúne muestras de la riqueza artística de nuestra Semana Santa y del Tesoro de las Hermandades y Cofradías Sevillanas.
Horas de visita:
De 10 a 14 y de 16 a 20, todos los días.
Precio de entrada: 15 pesetas; niños y estudiantes: 10 pesetas.

HOSPITAL DE LA CARIDAD. Del siglo XVII, fundado por Miguel de Mañara. Iglesia con famosos cuadros de Valdés Leal, Murillo y otras obras de arte. Altar mayor de Pedro Roldán.
Horas de visita:
De 10 a 12, en todo tiempo.
Verano, de 15 a 19.
Invierno, de 15 a 17,30.
Domingos y festivos, visita sólo por la tarde.
Precio de entrada: 15 pesetas.

TORRE DEL ORO. Torre almohade del siglo XIII, límite de las murallas sobre el río Guadalquivir. Hoy Museo de Marina.

PARQUE DE MARIA LUISA. Bellísimos jardines con numerosas glorietas. En él se encuentran los pabellones de la Exposición Iberoamericana y la monumental Plaza de España. En el que fue Palacio Renacimiento, en la Plaza de América, está instalado el Museo Arqueológico.
Horas de visita:
A los jardines, todo el día, gratuitamente.
Al Museo Arqueológico: de 9 a 14 y de 16 a 18, excepto lunes.
Precio de entrada: 10 pesetas.

CASA DE PILATOS. Palacio de los Duques de Medinaceli. Bellísimo ejemplar de estilo mudéjar (combinación de elementos árabes, góticos y platerescos).
Horas de visita:
Verano, de 9 a 13 y de 16 a 19. Invierno, de 10 a 13 y de 16 a 18.
Precio de entrada: 15 pesetas.

ARCHIVO GENERAL DE INDIAS. Antigua Casa Lonja, construida por Juan de Minjares según planos de Juan de Herrera, arquitecto de El Escorial. Aloja valiosos e interesantes documentos sobre el descubrimiento, conquista y colonización de América. Suntuosa escalera de la época de Carlos III.
Horas de visita:
Por grupos, a las 10, 11, 12 y 12,30 (días laborables).
Entrada gratuita.

AYUNTAMIENTO. Bellísimo ejemplar de estilo plateresco de la primera mitad del siglo XVI. Se puede visitar solicitando permiso, siendo gratuita la entrada.

MUSEO DE BELLAS ARTES. Instalado en el antiguo Convento de la Merced, felizmente adaptado a sus fines actuales. Aloja las más completas colecciones de Murillo y Valdés Leal, un Greco y obras de Zurbarán y otros maestros.
Horas de visita:
De 10 a 14 en todo tiempo. Además del horario de mañana, en marzo, abril, mayo y junio, de 16 a 17, en julio, agosto y septiembre, de 17 a 18. Cerrado los días festivos. Precio de entrada: 15 pesetas. Domingos gratis.

CASA DE LAS DUEÑAS. Palacio de los Duques de Alba, de estilo mudéjar. Actualmente cerrado al público.

BASILICA DE LA MACARENA. Suntuosa construcción moderna, donde se venera la famosa imagen de Nuestra Señora de la Esperanza (Macarena), talla atribuida a la Roldana. Junto a la Puerta de la Macarena, segmento de murallas romanas restauradas por los árabes.
Horas de visita:
De 9 a 13 y de 17 a 21.
Precio de entrada al Tesoro: 10 pesetas.

TEMPLO DEL GRAN PODER. Imagen de Nuestro Padre Jesús del Gran Poder, de Juan de Mesa, una de las obras más famosas de la imaginería sevillana.
Horas de visita:
De 8 a 13 y de 17 a 21,30.
Precio de entrada al Tesoro: 10 pesetas.

PALACIO ARZOBISPAL. Estilo barroco. Suntuosa escalera.

PALACIO DE SAN TELMO. Actualmente Seminario. Estilo barroco. Rica portada del siglo XVIII.

UNIVERSIDAD. Antigua Fábrica de Tabacos. Construida en el siglo XVIII.

COLUMNAS ROMANAS. Tres colosales fustes de columnas pertenecientes a un templo romano que se alzaba en ese lugar. Calle Mármoles.

IGLESIA DEL SALVADOR. Construida en el siglo XVIII sobre el emplazamiento de una mezquita. Modelo típico del barroco sevillano. Contiene las imágenes procesionales de Jesús de Pasión y San Cristóbal, de Martínez Montañés y el Cristo del Amor de Juan de Mesa.

CASA-PALACIO DE LA CONDESA DE LEBRIJA. Importante colección de mosaicos y otras obras notables procedentes de Itálica.

ANTIGUA UNIVERSIDAD. Anteriormente Casa Profesa de la Compañía de Jesús. Estilo Renacimiento. La iglesia conserva, entre otras obras de arte, el Cristo de los Estudiantes de Juan de Mesa.

IGLESIA DE SAN ESTEBAN. Estilo gótico-mudéjar. Cuadros de Zurbarán.

CONVENTO DE SAN LEANDRO. Retablos de Martínez Montañés.

IGLESIA DE SANTA CATALINA. Construcción mudéjar del siglo XIV sobre el emplazamiento de una antigua mezquita, de la que subsisten algunas arcas y el alminar.

CONVENTO DE SANTA INES. Estilo gótico-mudéjar. Buenos retablos y pinturas.

IGLESIA DE SAN MARCOS. Construcción de estilo gótico-mudéjar sobre el emplazamiento de una antigua mezquita de la que subsiste el bello alminar.

CONVENTO DE SANTA PAULA. Bellísima portada gótico-mudéjar con decoración de cerámica. En el interior de la iglesia obras de Martínez Montañés; azulejos notables.

IGLESIA DE SAN LUIS. Estilo barroco. Esculturas de Duque Cornejo.

IGLESIA DE SANTA MARIA LA BLANCA. Antigua sinagoga consagrada después al culto católico y transformada en el siglo XVII en la actual construcción barroca con profusión de yeserías. Entre las pinturas «La Cena» de Murillo.

IGLESIA DE OMNIUM SANCTORUM. Templo del siglo XIV. Bello ejemplar de alminar.

CONVENTO DE SAN CLEMENTE. De monjas cistercienses. Fundado por San Fernando. Artesonado mudéjar y azulejos del siglo XVI. Esculturas de Martínez Montañés y pinturas de Pacheco y Valdés Leal.

CONVENTO DE SANTA CLARA. Bellísimo compás. La iglesia tiene retablos de Martínez Montañés. En los jardines Torre de D. Fadrique, ejemplar de transición del románico al gótico.

LOS HERCULES. Columnas romanas procedentes del templo anteriormente citado, situadas en la Alameda.

IGLESIA DE SAN LORENZO. Retablo del altar mayor de Martínez Montañés. Notable pintura al fresco de la Virgen de Rocamador del siglo XIV.

CAPILLA DE SAN JOSE. Joya del arte barroco. Monumento Nacional.

IGLESIA DE SANTA MARIA MAGDALENA. Magnífico ejemplo del barroco. Pinturas murales de Lucas Valdés. Restos del primitivo templo mudéjar.

CAPILLA DEL ANTIGUO SEMINARIO. Estilo gótico-mudéjar. Retablo con tablas de Alejo Fernández. Monumento Nacional. Avenida Queipo de Llano, 19.

HOSPITAL DE LAS CINCO LLAGAS. Actualmente Hospital Provincial. Del siglo XVI. La iglesia fue construida por Hernán Ruiz. Plaza Macarena.

CAPILLA DEL PATROCINIO. Imagen del Cristo de la Expiración vulgarmente llamado «El Cachorro» de Ruiz Gijón, una de las obras más importantes de la imaginería sevillana. Calle Castilla, 164.

RUINAS DE ITALICA. A ocho kilómetros de Sevilla, junto al pueblo de Santiponce, las ruinas de la ciudad romana, con grandioso anfiteatro y bellos mosaicos. Patria de emperadores. A la entrada del pueblo, Monasterio de San Isidoro del Campo. En la iglesia, bellísimo retablo, obra cumbre de Martínez Montañés.
Horas de visita:
De marzo a octubre, de 9 a 19,30. De noviembre a febrero, de 9 a 17,30. Salida de autobuses del Paseo de Colón (Casa Luis).
Precio de entrada: 10 pesetas.

ENSEMBLE MONUMENTAL

LA CATHEDRALE. Sur l'emplacement de la Grande Mosquée des almohades, dont subsistent le Patio des Ablutions, la Porte du Pardon et la fameuse Giralda, on construisit la Cathédrale au XVe s., qui par ses dimensions, est la plus grande d'Espagne et la troisième du monde chrétien, et est un intéressant échantillon de l'art gothique. Son retable est le plus grand de toute la chrétienté. Riche trésor et nombreuses oeuvres d'art par toute la Cathédrale; peintures de Murillo, Goya, Pedro de Campaña, Luis de Vargas; sculptures de Martínez Montañés, Lorenzo Mercadante de Bretaña et autres.
Heures de visite:
Eté: de 10.30 à 12.30 et de 16 à 18.30.
Hiver: de 10.30 à 12.30 et de 15 à 17.30.
Prix d'entrée: 20 ptas.
La Giralda, minaret de l'ancienne mosquée est d'art almohade (XIIe s.) avec le corps de cloches de la Renaissance. Même horaire.
Prix d'entrée: 5 ptas.

ALCAZARES ROYAUX. Palais mudéjar du XIVe s. construit par Pierre I de Castille, sur les anciens palais musulmans dont subsiste le Patio del Yeso. Magnifiques, les Patios de las Doncellas et de las Muñecas, et le Salon d'Ambassadeurs. Edifications postérieures des siècles XV à XVIII. Merveilleux jardins de divers styles.
Heures de visite:
Eté: de 9 à 12.45 et de 16 à 18.45.
Hiver: de 9 à 12.45 et de 15 à 17.
Fermé: 1 janvier, 25 décembre, Vendredi Saint et Fête-Dieu.
Exposition Permanente du Patrimoine National. Jours fériés et dimanches, seulement le matin.
Prix d'entrée: 30 ptas.

QUARTIER DE SANTA CRUZ. Ancienne juiverie, c'est le quartier typique de Séville, avec la beauté spéciale du Callejón del Agua et la calle de la Pimienta, et les places de Santa Marta, Doña Elvira et Santa Cruz, avec la Cruz de Cerrajería, véritable dentelle de fer forcé du XVIIe s.

HOSPICE DES VENERABLES PRETRES ET MUSEE DE SEMAINE SAINTE. En plein quartier de Santa Cruz. L'église est de style baroque et conserve de remarquables oeuvres d'art. Très beau patio. Le Musée réunit des échantillons de la richesse artistique de notre Semaine Sainte et du Trésor des Confréries et Fraternelles Sévillanes.
Heures de visite:
De 10 à 14 et de 16 à 20, tous les jours.
Prix d'entrée: 15 ptas. Enfants et étudiants: 10 ptas.

HOPITAL DE LA CHARITE. Du XVIIe s. Fondé par Miguel de Mañara. Eglise avec fameux tableaux de Valdés Leal, Murillo et autres oeuvres d'art. Maître autel de Pedro Roldán.
Heures de visite:
De 10 à 12, en tout temps.
Eté: de 15 à 19.
Hiver: de 15 à 17.30.
Dimanches et jours fériés, seulement l'après-midi.
Prix d'entrée: 15 ptas.

TOUR DE L'OR. Tour almohade du XIIIe s. limite des murailles sur le fleuve Guadalquivir. Aujourd'hui, Musée de Marine.

PARC DE MARIA LUISA. Très beaux jardins avec nombreuses gloriettes. On y trouve les pavillons de l'Exposition Ibéroaméricaine et la monumentale Plaza de España. Dans ce qui fut Palais Renaissance, sur la Plaza de América, est installé le Musée Archéologique.
Heures de visite:
Aux jardins, toute la journée, gratuitement.
Au Musée Archéologique, de 9 à 14 et de 16 à 18, sauf le lundi.
Prix d'entrée: 10 ptas.

MAISON DE PILATOS. Palais des Ducs de Medinaceli. Très bel exemplaire de style mudéjar (combinaison d'éléments arabes, gothiques et plateresques).
Heures de visite:
Eté: de 9 à 13 et de 16 à 19.
Hiver: de 10 à 13 et de 16 à 18.
Prix d'entrée: 15 ptas.

ARCHIVES GENERALES DES INDES. Ancienne Casa Lonja. Construite par Juan de Minjares selon plans de Juan de Herrera, architecte de l'Escorial. Abrite de précieux et intéressants documents sur la découverte, conquête et colonisation d'Amérique. Somptueux escalier de l'époque de Charles III.
Heures de visite:
Par groupes, à 10, 11, 12 et 12.30 (jours ouvrables).
Entrée gratuite.

HOTEL DE VILLE. Très bel exemplaire de style plateresque de la première moitié du XVIe s. On peut visiter en demandant la permission, l'entrée étant gratuite.

MUSEE DES BEAUX ARTS. Installé dans l'ancien couvent de la Merced, bien adapté

à ses fins actuelles. Abrite les plus complètes collections de Murillo et Valdés Leal, un Greco et des oeuvres de Zurbarán et autres maîtres.
Heures de visite:
De 10 à 14 en tout temps. Outre l'horaire du matin, en mars, avril, mai et juin, de 16 à 17; juillet, août, septembre, de 17 à 18. Fermé les jours fériés.
Prix d'entrée: 15 ptas. Dimanches, entrée gratuite.

MAISON DE LAS DUEÑAS. Palais des Ducs d'Albe, de style mudéjar. Actuellement fermé au public.

BASILIQUE DE LA MACARENA. Somptueuse construction moderne, où l'on vénère la fameuse statue de Notre Dame de l'Espérance (Macarena), statue attribuée à la Roldana. Près de la Porte de la Macarena, segment de murailles romaines restaurées par les arabes.
Heures de visite:
De 9 à 13 et de 17 à 21.
Prix d'entrée au Trésor: 10 ptas.

TEMPLE DU GRAN PODER. Statue de Notre Père Jésus del Gran Poder de Juan de Mesa, une des oeuvres les plus fameuses de la statuaire sévillane.
Heures de visite:
De 8 à 13 et de 17 à 21.30.
Prix d'entrée au Trésor: 10 ptas.

PALAIS ARCHIEPISCOPAL. Style baroque. Escalier somptueux.

PALAIS DE SAN TELMO. Actuellement séminaire. Style baroque. Riche portique du XVIIIe s.

UNIVERSITE. Ancienne fabrique de Tabacs. Construite au XVIIIe s.

COLONNES ROMAINES. Trois fûts colossaux de colonnes appartenant à un temple romain qui se dressait à cet endroit. Calle Mármoles.

EGLISE DU SAUVEUR (El Salvador). Construite au XVIIIe s. sur l'emplacement d'une mosquée. Modèle typique du baroque sévillan. Contient les statues de procession de Jésus de Passion et Saint Christophe, de Martínez Montañés et le Christ de l'Amour de Juan de Mesa.

MAISON-PALAIS DE LA COMTESSE DE LEBRIJA. Importante collection de mosaïques et autres oeuvres remarquables provenant d'Italica.

ANCIENNE UNIVERSITE. Anciennement, maison Professe de la Compagnie de Jésus. Style Renaissance; l'église conserve, parmi d'autres oeuvres d'art, le Christ des Etudiants, de Juan de Mesa.

EGLISE DE SAN ESTEBAN (St. Etienne). Style gothico-mudéjar. Tableaux de Zurbarán.

COUVENT DE SAN LEANDRO (St. Léandre). Retables de Martínez Montañés.

EGLISE DE SANTA CATALINA (Ste. Catherine). Construction mudéjare du XIVe sur l'emplacement d'une ancienne mosquée, dont subsistent quelques arcades et le minaret.

COUVENT DE SANTA INES (Ste. Agnès). Style gothico-mudéjar. Bons retables et peintures.

EGLISE DE SAN MARCOS (St. Marc). Construction de style gothico-mudéjar sur l'emplacement d'une ancienne mosquée dont subsiste le beau minaret.

COUVENT DE SANTA PAULA (Ste. Paula). Très beau portique gothico-mudéjar avec décoration de céramique. A l'intérieur de l'église, oeuvres de Martínez Montañés; remarquables céramiques.

EGLISE DE SAN LUIS (St. Louis). Style baroque. Sculptures de Duque Cornejo.

EGLISE DE STE. MARIE LA BLANCHE. Ancienne synagogue consacrée ensuite au culte catholique et transformee au XVIIe s. en l'actuelle construction baroque avec profusion de plâtres. Parmi les peintures, «La Cène» de Murillo.

EGLISE DE OMNIUM SANCTORUM. Temple du XIVe s. Bel exemplaire de minaret.

COUVENT DE SAN CLEMENTE (St. Clément). De religieuses cisterciennes. Fondé par St. Ferdinand. Lambrissage mudéjar et faïences du XVIe s. Sculptures de Martínez Montañés et peintures de Pacheco et Valdés Leal.

COUVENT DE SANTA CLARA (Ste. Claire). Tres beau domaine. L'église a des retables de Martínez Montañés. Dans les jardins, Tour de D. Fadrique, exemplaire de transition du roman au gothique.

LOS HERCULES. Colonnes romaines provenant du temple déjà cité, situées sur l'Alameda.

EGLISE DE SAN LORENZO (St. Laurent). Retable du maître-autel de Martínez Montañés. Remarquable peinture à la fresque de la Vierge de Rocamador du XIVe s.

CHAPELLE DE SAN JOSE (St. Joseph). Joyau de l'art baroque. Monument National.

EGLISE DE SANTA MARIA MAGDALENA (Ste. Marie Madeleine). Magnifique exemplaire du baroque. Peintures murales de Lucas Valdés. Restes du primitif temple mudéjar.

CHAPELLE DE L'ANCIEN SEMINAIRE. Style gothico-mudéjar. Retable avec planches d'Alejo Fernández. Monument National. Avda. Queipo de Llano, 19.

HOSPITAL DE LAS CINCO LLAGAS (Hôpital des Cinq Plaies). Actuellement hôpital provincial. Du XVIe s. L'église fut construite par Hernan Ruiz. Plaza Macarena.

CAPILLA DEL PATROCINIO (Chapelle du Patronage). Statue du Christ de l'Expiration, vulgairement appelée «El Cachorro» de Ruiz Gijón une des oeuvres les plus impor-

tantes de la statuaire sévillane. Calle Castilla, 164.

RUINES D'ITALICA. A huit kilomètres de Séville, près du village de Santiponce, les ruines de la ville romaine avec grandiose amphithéâtre et belles mosaïques. Patrie d'empereurs. A l'entrée du village, Monastère de San Isidoro del Campo. Dans l'église, très beau retable, chef d'oeuvre de Martinez Montañés.
Heures de visite:
De mars à octobre, de 9 à 19.30. De novembre à février, de 9 à 17.30.
Départ d'autobus du Paseo de Colón (Casa Luis).
Prix d'entrée: 10 ptas.

MONUMENTS

THE CATHEDRAL. Built in the XV century on top of the Main Mosque of the Almohade Moors, of which remain the Patio of Abluciones, the Gate of the Perdon and the famous Giralda. It is the largest in Spain and the third in Christendom, being an interesting example of Gothic art. Its altarpiece is the largest in all Christendom. Rich treasure and numerous works of art throughout the Cathedral: paintings by Murillo, Goya, Pedro de Campaña, Luis de Vargas; sculptures by Martínez Montañés, Lorenzo Mercadante de Bretaña and others.
Visiting hours:
Summer, from 10:30 to 12:30 and 16 to 18:30.
Winter, from 10:30 to 12:30 and 15 to 17:30.
Entrance fee: 20 pesetas.
The Giralda, the minaret of the old mosque, is of Almohade Moorish art (XII century), with a bell section from the Renaissance. Same visiting hours.
Entrance fee: 5 pesetas.

REALES ALCAZARES. Christian - Moorish palace from the XIV century, built by Pedro I of Castille on top of the old Moslem palaces of which remains the Patio of Yeso. Beautiful Patios of the Doncellas and of the Muñecas and the Room of Embassadors. Buildings from the XV to XVIII centuries. Marvelous gardens of various styles.
Visiting hours:
Summer, from 9 to 12:45 and 16 to 18:45.
Winter, from 9 to 12:45 and 15 to 17.
Closed Jan. 1, Dec. 25, Good Friday and Corpus Christi. Permanent exposition of the National Patrimony. Holidays and Sundays, open only in the morning.
Entrance fee: 30 pesetas.

NEIGHBORHOOD OF SANTA CRUZ. Old Jewish neighborhood, the typical sector of Seville with the especially interesting Street of the Water and the street of the Pimienta and the plazas of Santa Marta, Doña Elvira and Santa Cruz with the Cross of Cerrajería, a true lace-like wrought iron piece from the XVII century.

HOSPITAL OF THE VENERABLE FATHERS AND THE HOLY WEEK MUSEUM. In the center of the neighborhood of Santa Cruz. The church is in Baroque style and contains notable works of art. Beautiful patio. Museum contains examples of the artistic wealth of our Holy Week and of the Treasure of the Hermandades and «Cofradías» of Seville.
Visiting hours:
From 10 to 14 and 16 to 20, every day.
Entrance fee: 15 pesetas; children and students: 10 pesetas.

HOSPITAL OF CHARITY. From the XVII century, founded by Miguel de Mañara. Church with famous paintings by Valdés Leal, Murillo and other works of art. Main altar by Pedro Roldán.
Visiting hours:
From 10 to 12, all year round.
Summer, from 15 to 19.
Winter, from 15 to 17:30.
Sundays and holidays, open only in the afternoon.
Entrance fee: 15 pesetas.

TOWER OF GOLD. XII century Almohade Moorisch tower, the end of the walls over the Guadalquivir river. Today, the Marine Museum.

MARIA LUISA PARK. Beautiful gardens with numerous monuments. Located here are the ibero-american Exposition and the Plaza de España. The Archaeological Museum is installed in what was the Renaissance Palace, in the Plaza de América.
Visiting hours:
To the gardens, all day, free of charge.
To the Archaeological Museum, from 9 to 14 and 16 to 18, except Mondays.
Entrance fee: 10 pesetas.

HOUSE OF PILATOS. Palace of the Dukes of Medinaceli. Beautiful example of Christian-Moorish style (combination of Arabic, Gothic and Plateresque elements).
Visiting hours:
Summer, from 9 to 13 and 1[illegible] to 19.
Winter, from 10 to 13 and 16 to 18.
Entrance fee: 15 pesetas.

GENERAL ARCHIVE OF THE INDIES. Old Casa Lonja, built by Juan de Minjares according to the plans of Juan de Herrera, the architect of El Escorial. It contains valuable and interesting documents on the discovery, conquest and colonization of América. Beautiful staircase from the period of Carlos III.
Visiting hours:
In groups, at 10, 11, 12 and 12:30 (week days).
Entrance free.

CITY HALL. Beautiful example of the Plateresque style from the first half of the XVI century. It can be visited by permission and entrance is free.

FINE ARTS MUSEUM. Installed in the old Convent of la Merced, well adapted to its present use. It contains the most complete collections of paintings by Murillo and Valdés Leal, one Greco and some by Zurbarán and other masters.
Visiting hours:
From 10 to 14, all year round. In addition, in March, April, May and June, from 16 to 17; in July, August and Sept., from 17 to 18. Closed holidays.
Entrance fee: 15 pesetas. Sundays: Entrance free.

HOUSE OF LAS DUEÑAS. Palace of the Dukes of Alba, in Christian-Moorish style. At present closed to the public.

BASILICA OF LA MACARENA. Beautiful modern construction, where the famous image of Our Lady of Hope (Macarena), a sculpture attributed to la Roldana, is worshipped. Next to the Door of the Macarena, a segment of Roman wall restored by the Arabs.
Visiting hours:
From 9 to 13 and 17 to 21.
Entrance fee to the Treasure Room: 10 pesetas.

TEMPLE OF THE GRAN PODER. Image of Our Father Jesús of Great Power, by Juan de Mesa, one of the most famous works in Seville imagery.
Visiting hours:
From 8 to 13 and 17 to 21:30.
Entrance fee to the Treasure Room: 10 pesetas.

PALACE OF THE ARCHBISHOP. Baroque style. Lovely staircase.

PALACE OF SAN TELMO. Present Seminary. Baroque style. Rich XVIII century entrance.

UNIVERSITY. Old Tobacco Factory. Built in the XVIII century.

ROMAN COLUMNS. Three Immense fusts of columns belonging to a Roman temple that was built here, in the street Mármoles.

CHURCH OF EL SALVADOR. Built in the XVIII century on top of a mosque. Typical example of the Baroque style of Seville. It contains the processional images of Jesús of Passion and San Cristóbal, by Martínez Montañés, and the Christ of Love by Juan de Mesa.

HOUSE-PALACE OF THE COUNTESS OF LEBRIJA. Important collection of mosaics and other notable works from Italy.

OLD UNIVERSITY. Previously the House of the Company of Jesús. Renaissance style. The church contains, among other works of art, the Christ of the Students by Juan de Mesa.

CHURCH OF SAN ESTEBAN. Gothic-Christian-Moorish style. Paintings by Zurbarán.

CONVENT OF SAN LEANDRO. Altarpieces by Martínez Montañés.

CHURCH OF SANTA CATALINA. XIV century Christian-Moorish construction built on top of an old mosque of which remain the beautiful minaret, and several arks.

CONVENT OF SANTA INES. Gothic-Christian-Moorish style, with good altarpieces and paintings.

CHURCH OF SAN MARCOS. Built in Gothic-Christian-Moorish style on top of an old mosque of which remains the minaret.

CONVENT OF SANTA PAULA. Very beautiful Gothic-Christian-Moorish entrance with ceramic decoration. Inside the church, works by Martínez Montañés and notable tiles.

CHURCH OF SAN LUIS. Baroque style. Sculptures by Duque Cornejo.

CHURCH OF SANTA MARIA LA BLANCA. Old synagogue later converted to Catholic worship and transformed in the XVII century into the present Baroque construction with a profusion of plaster work. Among its paintings, the «Supper» by Murillo.

CHURCH OF OMNIUM SANCTORUM. XIV century temple. Beautiful minaret.

CONVENT OF SAN CLEMENTE. Of the Cistercine Order. Founded by San Fernando. Christian-Moorish panelling and XVI century tiles. Sculptures by Martínez Montañés and paintings by Pacheco and Valdés Leal.

CONVENT OF SANTA CLARA. Very beautiful. The church has altarpieces by Martínez Montañés. In the gardens, the Tower of D. Fadrique, an example of the transition from the Romanic style to the Gothic.

LOS HERCULES. Roman columns from the fore-mentioned temple, located in la Alameda.

CHURCH OF SAN LORENZO. Main altarpiece by Martínez Montañés. Notable fresco of the Virgin of Rocamador from the XIV century.

CHAPEL OF SAN JOSE. A jewel in Baroque style. A National Monument.

CHURCH OF SANTA MARIA MAGDALENA. Magnificent example of the Baroque style. Mural paintings by Lucas Valdés. Remains of the original Christian-Moorish temple.

CHAPEL OF THE OLD SEMINARY. Gothic-Christian-Moorish style. Altarpiece with tablets by Alejo Fernández. National Monument. Avenida Queipo de Llano, 19.

HOSPITAL OF LAS CINCO LLAGAS. At present the Provincial Hospital. From the XVI century. The church was built by Hernán Ruiz. Plaza Macarena.

CHAPEL OF THE PATROCINIO. Image of the Christ of the Expiration, popularly called the «El Cachorro», by Ruiz Gijón, one of the most important works from the Seville school of imagery. Street Castilla, 164.

RUINS OF ITALICA. Eight kilometers from Seville, next to the town of Santiponce, the ruins of the Roman city, with a grand amphitheater and beautiful mosaics. Land of embassadors. At the entrance to the town, the Monastery of San Isidoro del Campo. In the church, a very beautiful altarpiece, a master work by Martínez Montañés.
Visiting hours:
From March to October, from 9 to 19:30. From November to February, from 9 to 17:30. Departure of buses from the Paseo de Colón (Casa Luis).
Entrance fee: 10 pesetas.

MONUMENTE

DIE KATHEDRALE. Auf dem Grundstück der Hauptmoschee der Almohaden, von der der Patio de Abluciones, die Puerta del Perdón und die berühmte Giralda erhalten blieben, erbaute man im XV. Jahrh. die Kathedrale, die das grösste Gotteshaus Spaniens und das drittgrösste der christlichen Welt darstellt. Sie is ein interessantes Beispiel des gotischen Baustils. Der Altaraufsatz ist der grösste der Christenheit. Kathedralschatz und zahlreiche Kunstwerke: Gemälde von Murillo, Goya, Pedro de Campaña, Luis de Vargas; Skulpturen von Martínez Montañés, Lorenzo Mercadante aus der Bretagne und anderen Bildhauern.
Besichtigungszeiten:
Sommer: 10.30-12.30 und 16.00-18.30 Uhr.
Winter: 10.30-12.30 und 15.00-17.30 Uhr.
Besichtigung: 20 Peseten.
Bei der Giralda, dem Minarett der alten Moschee handelt es sich um Almohadenkunst (XII. Jahrh.) mit einem Glockenstuhl im Renaissancestil.
Besichtigungszeiten: wie bei der Kathedrale.
Besichtigung: 5 Peseten.
ALKAZAR. Palast im Mudéjarstil aus dem XIV. Jahrh., den Pedro I. von Kastilien auf den alten muselmanischen Palästen, von denen noch der Patio del Yeso (Gipshof) besteht, erbauen liess. Schön sind der Patio de las Doncellas (Mädchenhof), der Patio de las Muñecas (Puppenhof) un der Salón de Embajadores (Botschaftersaal). Spätere Gebäude aus dem XV.—XVIII. Jahrh. Herrliche Gärten verschiedener Stile.
Besichtigungszeiten:
Sommer: 9.00-12.45 und 16.00-18.45 Uhr.
Winter: 9.00-12.45 und 15.00-17.00 Uhr.
Geschlossen: 1. Januar, 25. Dezember, Karfreitag und Fronleichnam.
Dauerausstellung des Patrimonio Nacional; an Sonn-und Feiertagen nur vormittags.
Besichtigung: 30 Peseten.
SANTA-CRUZ-STADVIERTEL. Altes Judenviertel, das heute ein typischer Stadtteil Sevillas ist. Besonders schön sind die Gasse Callejón del Agua und die Strasse de la Pimienta sowie die Plätze Santa Marta, Doña Elvira und Santa Cruz mit dem Cruz de Cerrajería, ein schmiedeeisernes Kreuz aus dem XVII. Jahrh., das einer Spitzenstickerei aus Eisen gleicht.
HOSPICIO DE LOS VENERABLES SACERDOTES UND KARWOCHEN-MUSEUM. Mitten im Santa-Cruz-Viertel. Die Kirche ist barock und beherbergt nennenswerte Kunstwerke. Sehr schöner Innenhof. Im Museum befinden sich Kunstschätze aus der Karwoche Sevillas und der Laienbrüderschaften.
Besichtigungszeiten:
10.00-14.00 und 16.00-20.00 Uhrtäglich.
Besichtigung: 15 Peseten; Kinder und Schüler: 10 Peseten.
HOSPITAL DE LA CARIDAD. Aus XVII. Jahrh; wurde von Miguel de Mañara gegründet. Kirche mit berühmten Gemälden von Valdés Leal, Murillo und andere Kunstwerke. Hauptaltaraufsatz von Pedro Roldán.
Besichtigungszeiten:
10.00-12.00 Uhr das ganze Jahr hindurch.
Sommer: 15.00-19.00 Uhr.
Winter: 15.00-17.30 Uhr.
An Sonn - und Feiertagen nur vormittags.
Besichtigung: 15 Peseten.
TORRE DEL ORO (Goldturm). Almohadenturm aus dem XII. Jahrh; Mauergrenze am Guadalquivir. Heute Marine-Museum.
MARIA-LUISA-PARK. Sehr schöne Gärten mit zahlreichen Lauben. Im Park befinden sich die Pavillons der Iberoamerikanischen Ausstellung und die monumentale Plaza de España. In dem ehemaligen Palacio Renacimiento auf der Plaza de América ist heute das Archäologische Museum untergebracht.
Besichtigungszeiten:
Die Gärten täglich; Besichtigung kostenlos.
Archäologisches Museum: 9.00-14.00 und 16.00-18.00 Uhr ausser montags.
Besichtigung: 10 Peseten.
CASA DE PILATOS. Palast der Herzöge von Medinaceli. Schönes Beispiel des Mudéjarstils (arabische, gotische und platereske Elemente).
Besichtigungszeiten:
Sommer: 9.00-13.000 und 16.00-19.00 Uhr.
Winter: 10.00-13.00 und 16.00-18.00 Uhr.
Besichtigung: 15 Peseten.
ARCHIVO GENERAL DE INDIAS. Alte Börse, die Juan de Minjares nach Plänen von Juan de Herrera, Architekt des Escorial, erbaute. Behütet wertvolle und interessante Dokumente über die Entdeckung, Eroberung und Besiedlung Amerikas. Prächtige Treppe aus der Zeit Karls III.
Besichtigungszeiten:
Gruppenweise 10.00; 11.00; 12.00 und 12.30 Uhr (werktags) gruppenweise.
Besichtigung: kostenlos.

RATHAUS. Sehr schönes Beispiel des plateresken Baustils aus der ersten Hälfte des XVI. Jahrh. Besichtigung auf Wunsch möglich, kostenlos.

MUSEUM DER SCHONEN KÜNSTE. Befindet sich im alten Kloster de la Merced, das seinem heutigen Zweck entsprechend eingerichtet wurde. Beherbergt die komplettesten Gemäldesammlungen von Murillo und Valdés Leal, einen Greco und Werke von Zurbarán und anderen Meistern.

Besichtigungszeiten:

10.00-14.00 Uhr. Ausser diesen Zeiten ist das Museum im März, April, Mai und Juni auch von 16.00-17.00 Uhr, im Juli, August und September von 17.00-18.00 Uhr geöffnet. An Feiertagen bleibt das Gebäude geschlossen.

Besichtigung: 15 Peseten; sonntags: kostenlos.

CASA DE LAS DUEÑAS. Palast der Herzöge von Alba. Mudéjarstil. Das Gebäude ist zur Zeit für das Publikum geschlossen.

BASILICA DE LA MACARENA. Prächtiges modernes Gebäude, in dem Nuestra Señora de la Esperanza, die Macarena (hoffnungsreiche Muttergottes) verehrt wird; es handelt sich hier um eine Madonnenfigur von der Roldana.

Neben der Puerta de la Macarena, Segment römischer Mauern, die von den 9.00-13.00 und 17.00-21.00 Uhr.

Besichtigungszeiten:

Arabern restauriert wurden.

Besichtigung der Schatzkammer: 10 Peseten.

TEMPLO DEL GRAN PODER. Kirche mit Christusstatue Nuestro Padre Jesús del Gran Poder von Juan de Mesa, die eines der berühmtesten Heiligenbildnisse Sevillas darstellt.

Besichtigungszeiten:

8.00-13.00 und 17.00-21.30 Uhr.

Besichtigung der Schatzkammer: 10 Peseten.

ERZBISCHOFSPALAST. Barocker Baustill. Prächtige Treppe.

PALACIO DE SAN TELMO. Heute Seminar. Barocker Baustil. Herrliches Portal aus dem XVIII. Jahrh.

UNIVERSITAT. Alte Tabakfabrik. Erbauung im XVIII. Jahrh.

ROMISCHE SAULEN. Drei riesige Säulenschäfte, die zu einem römischen Tempel gehörten, welcher sich hier in der Mármoles-Strasse erhob.

SALVADOR-KIRCHE. Wurde im XVIII. Jahrh. auf dem Grundstück einer Moschee erbaut. Typisches Beispiel des barocken Baustils in Sevilla. Enthält die Heiligenstatuen Jesús de Pasión und San Cristóbal von Martinez Montañés sowie Cristo del Amor von Juan de Mesa.

PALAST DER GRAFIN VON LEBRIJA. Mit bedeutender Mosaiksammlung und anderen nenneswerten Werken aus Itálica.

ALTE UNIVERSITAT. Ehemaliges Ordenshau des Jesuitenordens. Renaissancestil. Di Kirche behütet unter anderem den Crist de los Estudiantes (Christus der Studenten von Juan de Mesa.

SAN-ESTEBAN-KIRCHE. Baustil; gotisch Mudéjar. Gemälde von Zurbarán.

SAN-LEANDRO-KLOSTER. Altaraufsätze vo Martinez Montañés.

SANTA-CATALINA-KIRCHE. Mudéjarstil au dem XIV. Jahrh. Die Kirche wurde auf der Grundstück einer alten Moschee erbau von der noch einige Bogen und das Minare bestehen.

SANTA-INES-KLOSTER. Baustil: gotisch-Mu déjar. Gute Altaraufsätze und Gemälde.

SAN-MARCOS-KIRCHE. Baustil: gotisch-Mu déjar. Kirche auf dem Grundstück einer alte Moschee, von der das schöne Minare erhalten blieb.

SANTA-PAULA-KLOSTER. Sehr schönes Por tal im gotischen Mudéjarstil mit Keramikv erzierungen. Im Inneren der Kirche Werk von Martinez Montañés und nennenswert Fliesenarbeiten.

SAN-LUIS-KIRCHE. Barocker Baustil. Skulp turen von Duque Cornejo.

KIRCHE SANTA MARIA LA BLANCA. Alt Synagoge, die später geweiht und im XVI Jahrh. ihr heutiges Aussehen mit reicher Gipswerk erhielt. Unter den Gemälden be findet sich «Das Abendmahl» von Murill

KIRCHE OMNIUM SANCTORUM. Gottes haus dem XIV. Jahrh. mit einem schöne Minarett.

SAN-CLEMENTE-KLOSTER. Von Nonnen de Zisterzienserordens bewohnt. Wurde vo Fernando III. gegründet. Enthält ein Täfe werk im Mudéjarstil und Fliesen aus der XVI. Jahrh. Skulpturen von Martinez Mon tañés und Gemälde von Pacheco und Valdé Leal.

SANTA-CLARA-KLOSTER. Mit sehr schöner Atrium. Die Kirche enthält Altaraufsätze vo Martinez Montañés. In den Gärten Fadrique Turm, ein Beispiel aus der Übergangsze zwischen Romanik und Gotik.

LOS HERCULES. Römische Säulen aus vorh genannten Tempel, die sich in der Alamed befinden.

SAN-LORENZO-KIRCHE. Hauptaltaraufsa von Martinez Montañés. Bedeutende Fre skomalerei aus dem XIV. Jahrh. die Virge de Rocamador darstellend.

CAPILLA DE SAN JOSE. Juwel der barocke Kunst. Nationaldenkmal

KIRCHE SANTA MARIA MAGDALENA. Gros sartiges Beispiel des barocken Baustil Wandmalereien von Lucas Valdés. Überrest des ursprünglichen Tempels im Mudéjarst

KAPELLE DES ALTEN SEMINARS. Baust gotisch-Mudéjar. Altaraufsatz mit Gemälde auf Holz von Alejo Fernández. Nationa denkmal. Avenida Queipo de Llano, 1

HOSPITAL DE LAS CINCO LLAGAS. Heute Landeskrankenhaus. Das Gebäude stammt aus dem XVI. Jahrh. Die Kirche erbaute Hernán Ruiz. Plaza Macarena.

CAPILLA DEL PATROCINIO. Mit der Statue des sterbenden Christus, die im Volksmund unter dem Namen «El Cachorro» bekannt ist; ein Werk von Ruiz Gijón, das zu den bedeutendsten Heiligenbildnissen Sevillas zählt. Calle Castilla 164.

RUINEN VON ITALICA. 8 km. von Sevilla entfernt ruhen neben dem Dorf Santiponce die Ruinen der römischen Stadt mit einem grossen Amphitheater und schönen Mosaiken. Geburtsort römischer Kaiser. An der Einfahrt zum Dorf befindet sich das Kloster San Isidoro del Campo. In der Kirche ein sehr schöner Altaraufsatz von Martínez Montañés.

Besichtigungszeiten:
März—Oktober: 9.00-19.30 Uhr.
November—Februar: 9.00-17.30 Uhr.
Autobuses fahren vom Paseo de Colón (Casa Luis) ab.
Besichtigung: 10 Peseten.

HOTELES—HÔTELS HOTELS—HOTELS

Sevilla

ALFONSO XIII. San Fernando, 2. Telf. 22 28 50. H. L.
CRISTINA. Jardines Cristina, s/n. Telf. 22 66 80. H. L.
LUZ SEVILLA. Martín Villa, 4 y 6. Telf. 22 29 91. H. L.
COLON. José Canalejas, 1. Telf. 22 29 00. H. 1.ª A.
INGLATERRA. Plaza Nueva, 10. Telf. 22 49 70. H. 1.ª A.
LORIDA. Menéndez Pelayo, 47. Telf. 25 18 09 - 25 18 00. H. 1.ª A (apartamentos).
IO. Virgen de Luján, 18. Telf. 27 54 83. H. 1.ª A (apartamentos).
ESIDENCIA ALCAZAR. Menéndez Pelayo, 8. Telf. 23 19 91. H. 1.ª B.
ESIDENCIA BIARRITZ. Daoiz, 5. Telf. 22 08 53. H. 1.ª B.
ESIDENCIA DUCAL. P. Encarnación, 14. Telf. 21 51 07. H. 1.ª B.
LEMING. Sierra Nevada y Concepción, s/n. Telf. 25 07 89. H. 1.ª B.
ONTECARLO. Gravina, 53. Telf. 21 75 01-2. H. 1.ª B.
IZA. Reyes Católicos, 5. Telf. 21 54 04. H. 1.ª B.
TTE. Brasil, 7 y 9. Telf. 23 18 88. H. 1.ª B.
A RABIDA. Castelar, 24. Telf. 22 09 60. H. 1.ª B.
ARRITZ. Martín Villa, 3. Telf. 22 67 95. H. 2.ª.
CECIL ORIENTE. Plaza Nueva, 8. Telf. 22 29 30. H. 2.ª.
HOSTERIA INTERNACIONAL. Aguilas, 15. Telf. 21 32 04-06-07. H. 2.ª.
FRANCIA. Méndez Nuñez, 7. Telf. 22 29 40. H. 2.ª.
LYON. Vidrio, 15. Telf. 25 56 33. H. 2.ª.
RESIDENCIA MURILLO. Lope de Rueda, 3. (Barrio de Santa Cruz). Telf. 21 60 95. H. 2.ª.
PARIS. San Pablo, 33. Telf. 22 28 60. H. 2.ª.
SIMON. García de Vinuesa, 21. Telf. 22 66 60-9. H. 2.ª.
BRISTOL. San Eloy, 7. Telf. 22 29 70. H. 3.ª.
RESIDENCIA JENTOFT. Benidorm, 2. Telf. 22 09 81. H. 3.ª.
LOZANO. Muñoz Olivé, 9. Telf. 22 40 60 y 21 35 55. H. 3.ª.
RESIDENCIA NUEVO SUIZO. Azofaifo, 6. Telf. 22 49 10-9. H. 3.ª.
ROMA. Gravina, 49 y 51. Telf. 22 89 49 y 22 00 04. H. 3.ª.
SUIZA. Carlos Cañal, 5. Telf. 22 08 13. H. 3.ª.

Alcalá de Guadaira

OROMANA. Pinares, s/n. Telf. 86. H. 1.ª B.

Dos Hermanas

MOTEL CLUB DEL CAMPO. Carretera Madrid-Cádiz, Km. 554. Telf. 58 y 474. H. 2.ª.

Ecija

CENTRAL. Plaza de España. Valderrama, s/n. Telf. 56 y 14. H. 3.ª.
RESIDENCIA SANTIAGO. Ctra. Madrid-Cádiz. Km. 455. H. 3.ª.

PENSIONES—PENSIONS BOARDING HOUSES—PENSIONEN

Sevilla

HOSTAL ATENAS. Caballerizas, 1. Telf. 21 80 47-8. P. L.
HOSTAL BETIS. Betis, 67. P. L.
HOSTAL OTTEI. Felipe II. P. L.
HOSTAL EL PARAISO. Gravina, 23. Telf. 21 79 17. P. L.
HOSTAL SIERPES. Corral del Rey, 18. Telf. 22 49 48-9. P. L.
HOSTAL TOLEDO. Santa Teresa, 13. Telf. 21 53 42. P. L.
HOSTAL ZAIDA. San Roque, 28. Telf. 21 11 38. P. L.
HABITACIONES ASTORIA. Mateo Alemán, 5. Telf. 21 29 05. P. 1.ª.
HOSTAL LA CAMPANA. Javier Lasso de la Vega, 2. Telf. 21 74 00. P. 1.ª.

CAPITOL. Zaragoza, 74. Telf. 21 24 41. P. 1.ª.
HOSTAL CASA CALVILLO. General Polavieja, 1 y 3. Telf. 22 88 54-5. P. 1.ª
LOS CORRALES. General Polavieja, 19. Telf. 21 36 23. P. 1.ª.
HOSTERIA DEL LAUREL. Plaza de los Venerables, 5. Telf. 22 38 66. P. 1.ª.
HOSTAL LISBOA. San Eloy, 11. Telf. 22 14 20. P. 1.ª.
HOSTAL MALAGA. O'Donnell, 9. Telf. 21 36 18. P. 1.ª.
HOSTAL DEL PRADO. Avenida de Málaga, 6. Telf. 23 19 76. P. 1.ª.
HABITACIONES PUERTO RICO. Rioja, 13. Telf. 21 36 01. P. 1.ª.
HOSTAL ROM. Zaragoza, 22. Telf. 22 88 00-9. P. 1.ª.
HOSTAL SEVILLA. O'Donnell, 20. Telf. 22 58 97. P. 1.ª.
VILLA ADELA. Avenida de Barbolla, 65. Telf. 23 13 73. P.ª. 1.ª.
ALVERTOS. Miguel de Cervantes, 4. Telf. 22 49 13. P. 2.ª.
CASA MANOLO. Pajes del Corro, 29. Telf. 21 16 47 y 22 81 26. P. 2.ª.
LA CASTELLANA. Gamazo, 17. Teléfono 22 08 94-5. P. 2.ª.
CASTI. Bailén, 50. Telf. 22 35 20. P. 2.ª.
CLARINES. Trastamara, 29. Telf. 21 65 98. P. 2.ª.
DUQUE. Trajano, 15. P. 2.ª.
ESPADAFOR. Avenida de la Cruz del Campo, 11. Telf. 25 49 19 y 25 85 53. P. 2.ª.
ESPAÑOLA. San Eloy, 21. Telf. 22 11 09. P. 2.ª.
FABIAN-ESPAÑA. Méndez Núñez, 11. Telf. 22 54 05. P. 2.ª.
FELIPE II. Felipe II, 13. Telf. 23 12 77. P. 2.ª.
LONDRES. San Pedro Mártir, 1. Telf. 21 28 96. P. 2.ª.
MONREAL. Rodrigo Caro, 10. Telf. 21 54 14. P. 2.ª.
HOSTAL NEVADA. Gamazo, 26. Telf. 22 53 40. P. 2.ª.
NORTE. San Bernardo, 44. Telf. 25 56 27. P. 2.ª.
PUERTA REAL. Gravina, 22. Telf. 22 66 81-2. P. 2.ª.
SAEZ. Plaza de Curtidores, 6. Telf. 25 28 31. P. 2.ª.
SAN JOSE. Miguel de Cervantes, 6. Telf. 22 25 27. P. 2.ª.
HABITACIONES TORRE DEL ORO. Paseo de Colón, s/n. Telf. 21 50 05. P. 2.ª.
VENEZUELA. Tintes, 19. Telf. 25 73 10. P. 2.ª.
VIRGEN DE LOS REYES. Alvarez Quintero, 51 y 53. Telf. 21 48 51. P. 2.ª.

Ecija

HOSTAL CIUDAD EL SOL. Miguel de Cervantes, 42. Telf. 410. P. 1.ª.

Morón de la Frontera

HOSPEDAJE SAN AGUSTIN. Gral. Franco, 2
Telf. 332. P. 2.ª.

ACAMPAMENTOS TURISTICOS
CAMPINGS TOURISTIQUES
TOURIST CAMPING
CAMPINGPLÄTZE

DOS HERMANAS. «Giralda». 14 Km. de Sevilla (carretera de Cádiz).
DOS HERMANAS. «Wilson», 12 Km. de Sevilla (carretera de Cádiz).
SEVILLA. «Sevilla». 6 Km. de Sevilla (carretera de Córdoba).
DOS HERMANAS. «Motel Country Club» 12 Km. (carretera de Cádiz).

RESTAURANTES
RESTAURANTS
RESTAURANTS—RESTAURANTS

Sevilla

LOS ALCAZARES. Miguel Mañara, 10.
BAR LUIS. Paseo de Colón, 6.
CASA MANOLO. Avenida de María Luis
COLISEO. Avenida Queipo de Llano, 46.
EL BODEGON TORRE DEL ORO. Santander, 25.
GRAN ALMIRANTE. Plaza de Cristo de Burgos.
HOSTERIA DEL LAUREL. Plaza de los Venerables, 5.
HOSTERIA INTERNACIONAL. Aguilas, 1
HOSTERIA DEL PRADO. Estación de Autobuses.
LA COCHERA. Menéndez Pelayo, 42.
LA RAZA. Avenida de María Luisa.
LOS CORALES. Sierpes, 102.
LOS MONOS. Paseo de la Palmera.
PASAJE ANDALUZ. Sierpes, 82.
RIO GRANDE. Betis, 70.
BAR PUERTO. Betis, 59.
MARCELINO. Carretera de Cádiz.
VENTA RUIZ. Carretera de Cádiz.
PISCINAS SEVILLA. Avenida Ciudad Jard (verano).
CERVECERIA ESPAÑOLA. Tetuán, 39.
EL BARRIL. Tomás de Ibarra, 34.
EL MESON. Dos de Mayo, 26.
LA ISLA. Arfe, 24.
LOS QUINTERO. Alvarez Quintero, 29.
CASA PEINADO. Tarifa, 2.
CASA COBO. Menéndez Pelayo, 5.
MALAGA. O'Donnell, 9.
EL BURLADERO. José Canalejas, 1.
LIBANO. Avda. de Haití.
BILINDO. Paseo de las Delicias.
CASA CALVILLO. Sierpes, 74.
EL TROPICAL. Campana, 3.

A PONDEROSA. Plaza del Capitán Santiago Cortés (Gran Plaza).
A PUNTA DEL DIAMANTE. Avda. José Antonio, 31.
URIA. Avda. de Málaga.
ENTA DE LOS REYES. Ctra. de Cádiz, Km. 537.
LFONSO. Plaza de América.
OLON. Paseo de Colón, 2.
L «9». Menéndez y Pelayo, 42.
A MARINA. Paseo de Colón, 15.
AS MARAVILLAS. Amor de Dios, 37.
AS SIETE PUERTAS. Amor de Dios, 66.
OS GABRIELES. Plaza de la Legión, 1.
AVARROS. Sierpes, 25.
AVARROS. Gallegos, 23.
ASAJE DE LAS NAVAS. San Pablo, 13.
INEDA. Asunción, 43.
ENTA ANDALUCIA.
ENTA EL CRUCE. Autopista de San Pablo.
ICENTE. Tomás de Ibarra, 22.
ASA REMESAL. Ctra. Carmona, 34.
L «8». Plaza del Pozo Santo.
STACION. Plaza de Armas (Estación de Córdoba).
STACION SAN BERNARDO. (Estación de Cádiz).

Alcalá de Guadaira

IONTECARMELO. Carretera Sevilla-Málaga.
L PINO. Carretera Sevilla-Málaga.

El Arahal

OS TRES GATOS. Carretera Sevilla-Málaga.

Cabezas de San Juan

Cruce N-IV con la de Villamartín).
ENTA DE REINA. Carretera Madrid-Cádiz.
ENTA GALVEZ. Carretera Madrid-Cádiz.

Carmona

ASA CARMELO. San Pedro (travesía).
ASA GAMERO. San Pedro (travesía).
ASA CHACON. San Pedro (travesía).
A REJA. San Pedro (travesía).
L POTRO. San Pedro (travesía).

EL Cuervo

EVILLA-BETIS. Carretera Madrid-Cádiz.
ENTA MANOLO. Carretera Madrid-Cádiz, Km. 613,7.

Dos Hermanas

ENTA DIEGO. Carretera Sevilla-Cádiz, Km. 557.
OTEL CLUB. Carretera de Sevilla.

Estepa

EL PARAISO. Carretera Sevilla-Málaga.
NUEVO COLON. Carretera Sevilla-Málaga.

Ecija

M. CARMONA ESTEVEZ. Choza José María.
HERRERA MORENO. Plaza de España.
SILVA MARTIN. Carretera General.

Osuna

MESON DEL DUQUE. Plaza España.
LAS VEGAS. Carretera Sevilla-Málaga.

Los Palacios

EL DESEMBARCO. Travesía Carretera Madrid-Cádiz.

El Ronquillo

CASA PACO. Travesía Carretera Sevilla-Gijón.
CASA MATY. Travesía Carretera Sevilla-Gijón.
EL RONQUILLO. Carretera Sevilla-Gijón-Estación Servicio.

Sanlúcar la Mayor

VENTA PAZOS. Carretera Sevilla-Huelva.

ESPECIALIDADES GASTRONOMICAS

Gazpacho andaluz.
Pescado frito variado.
Pavías de bacalao.
Lomo de cerdo con manteca.
Sábalo.
Albures del Guadalquivir a la brasa y al horno.
Cola de toro guisada.
Es típico el servicio de «tapas» de cocina en todos los bares, que comprenden una extensa gama de pequeñas comidas. Y como complemento las aceitunas sevillanas, las más famosas de España.
Entre los dulces procede mencionar:
Yemas de San Leandro (que se venden en el convento de San Leandro, y en todas las confiterías).
Yemas de «El Ecijano», en Ecija.
Bizcotelas de Alcalá de Guadaira.
Mostachones de Utrera.
Polvorones y mantecados de Estepa, de gran consumo en toda España en las fiestas de Navidad.
Tortas de aceite de Castilleja de la Cuesta.

VINOS

La provincia de Sevilla tiene dos grandes zonas vinícolas: la de Villanueva del Ariscal, Benacazón, Pilas, de vinos blancos, semejantes a los del Condado y la de Lebrija, de vinos blancos de alta graduación que contribuyen en gran medida a la elaboración de los afamados vinos de Jerez.

El consumo general es de vinos de Jerez, del Puerto de Santa María; de manzanilla, de Sanlúcar de Barrameda, y de vinos del Condado (Huelva).

SPECIALITES GASTRONOMIQUES

Gazpacho andalou.
Friture variée de poisson.
«Pavias» de morue.
Filet de porc à la graisse.
Alose.
Cabot du Guadalquivir (albur) à la braise et au four.
Queue de taureau mijotée.
Le service de «tapas» dans les bars est typique, et comprend une vaste gamme de petits repas. Et, comme complément, les olives sévillanes, les plus fameuses d'Espagne.
Parmi les douceurs, il convient de mentionner: Yemas de San Leandro (jaunes d'oeuf) qui se vendent au couvent de San Leandro et dans toutes les confiseries.
Yemas de «El Ecijano» à Ecija.
Bizcotelas de Alcalá de Guadaira.
Mostachones de Utrera.
Polvorones et mantecados de Estepa, que l'on consomme beaucoup en Espagne à la Noël.
Tortas de aceite (tourtes à l'huile) de Castilleja de la Cuesta.

VINS

La province de Séville a deux grandes zones vinicoles; celle de Villanueva del Ariscal, Benacazón, Pilas, aux vins blancs semblables à ceux du Condado et celle de Lebrija, aux vins blancs de haute graduation qui contribuent en grande partie à l'élaboration des fameux vins de Jerez.

La consommation générale est de vins de Jerez, du Puerto de Santa María; de manzanilla de Sanlúcar de Barrameda, et de vins du Condado (Huelva).

FOOD SPECIALTIES

Andalusian Gazpacho.
Variety of fried fish.
«Pavias» of codfish.
Pork chine with lard.
Shad.
Dace from the Guadalquivir, roasted or baked
Stewed bull's tail.
It is customary in bars to serve «tapas» or hors d'oeuvres that include a large range of small meals. In addition, the Seville olives, the most famous in Spain.
In the line of sweets, we must mention:
Candied egg yolks of San Leandro (sold in the convent of San Leandro and in all bakeries).
«El Ecijano» candied egg yolks from Ecija.
«Bizcotelas» from Alcalá de Guadaira.
«Mostachones» from Utrera.
«Polvorones» and «mantecados» from Estepa, popular all over Spain at Christmas
«Tortas de aceite» from Castilleja de la Cuesta

WINES

The province of Seville has two large wine producing areas: in Villanueva del Arisca Benacazón, Pilas, that produce white wines similar to those from Condado and in Lebrija, with high grade white wines that ar used a great deal in the production of th famous wines of Jerez.

Jerez or sherry is used for general consumptior from the Puerto de Santa María, as wall a «manzanilla» wine from Sanlúcar de Barrameda, and the wines from Condado (Huelva).

GASTRONOMISCHE SPEZIALITÄTEN

Gazpacho andaluz = *Kalte Suppe aus Brotkrumen, mit Ol, Essig, Knoblauch, Zwiebel und geschmittenen Gurken.*
Pescado frito variado = *Gebratene Fische*
Pavías de bacalao = *Klösse aus Stockfisch*
Lomo de cerdo con manteca = *Schweinelendenbraten.*
Sábalo = *Alsen (Art Sardinen).*
Albures del Guadalquivir a la brasa y al horno = *Auf dem Kohlenfeuer oder im Ofen gebratene Weissfische.*
Cola de toro guisado = *Gekochter Ochsenschwanz.*
In den Bars werden hier zum Wein die typischen «tapas» *gereicht, die schon fast klein Mahlzeiten ausmachen; nicht zu vergesse sind die Oliven aus Sevilla, die berühmteste aus ganz Spanien.*
Von den Zuckerbäckereien sind zu nenner
Yemas de San Leandro.
Aus Eidotter und Zuckerschleim, das in San-Leandro-Kloster und in allen Konditoreien verkauft wird.
Yemas de «El Ecijano» *aus Ecija.*
Bizcotelas = *Feines Zuckerbrot aus Alcalá de Guadaira.*
Mostachones = *Kleine Marzipan-, Mandelkuchen aus Utrera.*

ılvorones *und* mantecados *aus Estepa, die zum Weihnachtsfest in ganz Spanien verkauft werden.*
ırtas de aceite = *Olkuchen aus Castilleja de la Cuesta.*

WEINE

der Provinz Sevilla gibt es zwei grosse Weingebiete: Das von Villanueva del Ariscal, Benacazón und Pilas, das Weissweine hervorbringt, die denen aus dem zweiten Weingebiet Condado und Lebrija ähneln. Diese Weissweine haben einen hohen Alkoholgehalt und tragen in grossem Masse zur Herstellung des Sherry bei.
ı allgemeinen trinkt man hier Sherry aus Puerto de Santa María und Manzanilla aus Sanlúcar de Barrameda sowie Weine aus dem Condado (Huelva).

CAFETERIAS—CAFETERIES CAFETERIAS—CAFES

CAPULCO. Amor de Dios, 25.
SUNCION. Asunción, 39.
ATUNAMBU. Ronda de Capuchinos, 1.
ORREOS. Avda. Queipo de Llano, 38.
RALDA. Mateos Gago, 1.
OLISEO. Avda. Queipo de Llano, 46.
.UB 22. Habana, 8.
STIVAL. Avda. Queipo de Llano, 42.
REDO. Sierpes, 102.
RAN ALMIRANTE. Plaza del Cristo de Burgos.
S VEGAS. Alemanes, 7.
REJA. Santa María de Gracia, 15.
AVARRO. Sierpes, 25.
JRIA. Avda. de Cádiz, 2.
VIERA. Campana, 8.
IRIN. Asunción (pista de baile).
.UB ALAZAN. Juan Sebastián Elcano, 21. (pista de baile).
S CANDILES. General Polavieja, 21.
ZA. Reyes Católicos, 5.
TORIL. Arjona, 6.
LY. San Jacinto, 120.
AMI. María Josefa Segovia, 44.
ALA. Imagen, 8.

LIBRERIAS—LIBRAIRIES BOOK SHOPS—BUCHHANDLUGEN

3RERIA ABAD. Menéndez Pelayo, 23.
3RERIA ARGENTINA. Avenida R. Argentina, 14.
3RERIA ATLANTIDA. Sierpes, 60.
3RERIA BALLESTEROS. Feria, 170.
3RERIA DEL CARMEN. Regina, 24.
SA DOMINGO DE CASO. Lagar, 8.
3RERIA CASAS. Asunción, 37.
LIBRERIA CATOLICA. Tetuán, 11.
LIBRERIA DEMAR. El Greco, 10.
LIBRERIA MIGUEL ESCANDON. Callao, 8.
LIBRERIA FERRER. Sierpes, 5.
LIBRERIA DELICIAS. José Maluquer, 13.
PAPELERIA GRAN PLAZA. Marqués de Pikman, 1.
LIBRERIA ANTONIO GUERRERO. Avenida Santa Cecilia, 3.
LIBRERIA EULOGIO DE LAS HERAS. Sierpes, 13.
LIBRERIA ANTONIO HERRERA. García de Vinuesa, 36.
LIBRERIA IMPERIAL. Pasaje Comercial «Gran Plaza».
LIBRERIA PASCUAL LAZARO. Francos, 43-47.
LIBRERIA MARIA AUXILIADORA. María Auxiliadora, 18.
LIBRERIA MARILINA. Echegaray, 1.
LIBRERIA MARIN VIZCAINO. Guadiana, 26-2.º.
LIBRERIA SAN ELOY. S. Eloy, 23.
LIBRERIA HIJOS DE A. PADURA. Cerrajería, 7
LIBRERIA PORTACELI. Avenida Eduardo Dato, 10.
PAPELERIA RAIMUNDO BLANCO. Falange Española, 5.
LIBRERIA REINA. Mateos Gago, 8.
LIBRERIA RIOS. Fray Isidoro de Sevilla, 1.
LIBRERIA EL ROSARIO DE ORO. Sagasta, 28-30.
LIBRERIA RELIGIOSA EL SALVADOR. Plaza del Salvador, 23.
LIBRERIA SANCHEZ. Sinaí, 22.
LIBRERIA SAN JOSE. Francos, 25.
LIBRERIA SAN PABLO. San Pablo, 33.
LIBRERIA SANZ. Sierpes, 90. Apartado 2.
LIBRERIA EL SOL. Jesús del Gran Poder, 55.
LIBRERIA SOTO. Sierpes, 55.
LIBRERIA TARSIS. Méndez Núñez, 21.
LIBRERIA VALENTIN. Amparo, 9-c.
LIBRERIA VALVERDE. Francos, 27.
LIBRERIA LUISA VAZQUEZ SUAREZ. Afán de Ribera, 77.
LIBRERIA WILSONS. Asunción, 58.

CORREOS, TELEFONOS Y TELEGRAFOS

CORREOS. Avenida Queipo de Llano, 40. Telf. 22 88 80.
Lista: de 9 a 13 y de 16 a 18 días laborables, y de 10 a 12, domingos y festivos.
TELEFONOS. Plaza Nueva, 3.
Información 003.
Conferencias interurbanas 009.
Teléfonos públicos de medidor automático: ficha 2 pesetas, para tres minutos.
TELEGRAFOS. Avenida Queipo de Llano, 40. Telf. 22 73 54. Sucursales o Estafetas de Correos y Telégrafos: San Jacinto (Triana),

Avenida de la Raza (Puerto) y Avda. de Cádiz.

POSTES, TELEPHONES ET TELEGRAPHES

POSTES. Avda. Queipo de Llano, 40. Telf. 22 88 80.
Poste restante: de 9 à 13 et de 16 à 18 jours ouvrables et de 10 à 12, dimanches et jours fériés.
TELEPHONES. Plaza Nueva, 3. Information 003.
Communications interurbaines: 009.
Téléphones publics à compteur automatique: fiche 2 ptas. pour trois minutes.
TELEGRAPHES. Avda. Queipo de Llano, 40. Telf. 22 73 54, succursales ou estafettes de courriers et télégraphes: San Jacinto (Triana), Avda. de la Raza (port) et Avda. de Cádiz.

POST OFFICES TELEPHONE AND TELEGRAPH

POST OFFICE. Avda. Queipo de Llano, 40. Telf. 22 88 80. Open from 9 to 13 and from 16 to 18 weekdays, and from 10 to 12, Sundays and holidays.
TELEPHONE OFFICE. Plaza Nueva, 3. Information: 003.
Interurban calls: 009. Public phones use 2 peseta tokens. for three minutes.
TELEGRAPH OFFICE. Avda. Queipo de Llano, 40. Telf. 22 73 54.
Branches of Telegraph and Post Offices: San Jacinto (Triana), Avda. de la Raza (Puerto) and Avda. de Cádiz.

POST—, FERNSPRECH— UND TELEGRAPHENAMT

CORREOS (Postamt). Avenida Queipo de Llano 40. Telf. 22 88 80. Postlagernde Briege: werktags von 9.00 — 13.00 und von 16.00 — 18.00 Uhr; sonn— und feiertags von 10.00 — 12.00 Uhr.
TELEFONOS (FERNSPRECHAMT). Plaza Nueva 3.
Information 003.
Ferngespräche 009.
Fernsprechzellen: 2—Peseten—Münzen für Gespräche von 3 Minuten.
TELEGRAFOS (TELEGRAPHENAMT). Avda. Queipo de Llano 40. Telf. 22 73 54. Zweigstellen oder Nebenpostämter: San Jacinto (Triana), Avenida de la Raza (Hafen) und Avda. de Cádiz.

CENTROS OFICIALES CENTRES OFFICIELS OFFICIAL CENTERS STAATLICHE AMTSSTELLEN

DELEGACION PROVINCIAL DE INFORMACION Y TURISMO. Avenida Queipo d Llano, 13. Telf. 22 89 90.
OFICINAS DE INFORMACION TURISTICA Avenida Queipo de Llano, 13. Telf. 22 14 04
OFICINA MUNICIPAL DE TURISMO. Alcázar, Puerta del León. Telf. 22 95 74.
GOBIERNO CIVIL. Plaza de España. Tel 23 19 71.
GOBIERNO MILITAR. Plaza de España. Tel 23 19 66.
AYUNTAMIENTO. Plaza Nueva, 1. Tel 21 28 00.

TELEFONOS DE URGENCIA

Casas de Socorro

Alhóndiga, 34. Telf. 22 32 82.
Almirante Apodaca, 2. Telf. 22 32 82.
Marqués de Nervión. Telf. 25 79 34.
Menéndez Pelayo, 2. Telf. 23 46 67.
Rosario, 15. Telf. 22 47 60.
San Jacinto, 35. Telf. 33 38 44.
Médico de urgencia. Telf. 25 80 06.

Policía

JEFATURA SUPERIOR. Plaza Gavidia. Te 21 29 23.
Llamada a la Policía. Telf. 091.

Objetos perdidos

Almansa, 23. Telf. 22 48 65.

TELEPHONES D'URGENCE

Dispensaires

Alhóndiga, 34. Telf. 22 32 82.
Almirante Apodaca, 2. Telf. 22 32 82.
Marqués de Nervión. Telf. 25 79 34.
Menéndez Pelayo, 2. Telf. 23 46 67.
Rosario, 15. Telf. 22 47 60.
San Jacinto. Telf. 33 38 44.
Médecin d'urgence. Telf. 25 80 06.

Police

DIRECTION SUPERIEURE. Plaza Gavidi Telf. 21 29 23.
Appel à la police: Telf. 091.

Objets perdus

Almansa, 23. Telf. 22 48 65.

EMERGENCY TELEPHONES

Emergency First Aid

Alhóndiga, 34. Telf. 22 32 82.
Almirante Apodaca, 2. Telf. 22 32 82.
Marqués de Nervión. Telf. 25 79 34.
Menéndez Pelayo, 2. Telf. 23 46 67.
Rosario, 15. Telf. 22 47 60.
San Jacinto. Telf. 33 38 44.
Doctor on call. Telf. 25 80 06.

Police

POLICE STATION. Plaza Gavidia. Telf. 212923.
Emergency calls. 091.

Lost and Found

Almansa, 23. Telf. 22 48 65.

WICHTIGE FERNSPRECHNUMMERN

Unfallstationen

Alhóndiga, 34. Telf. 22 32 82.
Almirante Apodaca 2. Telf. 22 32 82.
Marqués de Nervión. Telf. 25 79 34.
Menéndez Pelayo 2. Telf. 23 46 67.
Rosario 15. Telf. 22 47 60.
San Jacinto. Telf. 33 38 44.
Dienstbereiter Arzt: Telf. 25 80 06.

Polizeiamt

JEFATURA SUPERIOR (Oberpolizeiamt). Plaza Gavidia. Telf. 21 29 23. Polizei-Rufnummer 091.

Verlorene Gegenstände

Almansa 23. Telf. 22 48 65.

AGENCIAS DE VIAJES
AGENCES DE VOYAGES
TRAVEL AGENCIES
REISEBÜROS

ATESA-MARSANS. Avenida Queipo de Llano, 5. Telf. 21 41 93.
VIAJES ALHAMBRA. Santo Tomás, 1. Telf. 21 29 23.
VIAJES AYMAR (AMERICAN EXPRESS). Avenida Queipo de Llano, 46. Telfs. 22 39 82 y 22 82 49.
VIAJES BAKUMAR. República Argentina, 19. Telf. 22 66 20.
VIAJES BONANZA. García de Vinuesa, 3. Telfs. 22 20 74 y 22 77 24.
VIAJES CYRASA. Plaza Nueva, 14. Telfs. 22 92 23 y 21 83 74.
VIAJES ECUADOR. Plaza del Duque, 7. Telf. 21 78 56-7.
VIAJES HISPANIA. Avenida Queipo de Llano, 44. Telf. 22 45 38.
VIAJES INTERNACIONAL EXPRESO, S. A. Alemanes, 3. Telf. 21 38 28.
VIAJES MELIA, S. A. Avenida de José Antonio, 29. Telfs. 22 35 42 y 22 59 81.
VIAJES SOCIALTUR, S. A. Hernando Colón, 6. Telfs. 21 15 79 y 22 33 07.
VIAJES UNIVERSAL, S. A. Mateos Gago, 2. Telf. 21 65 02-27.
WAGONS-LITS-COOK. Avenida de José Antonio, 12. Telfs. 22 59 20 y 22 81 69.
ASTES (ASOCIACION SEGURO TURISTICO ESPAÑOL). Delegación: Plaza de Calvo Sotelo, 6. Telf. 22 81 73. Informes: Oficina de Información de la Subsecretaría de Turismo y Agencias de Viajes.

AGENCIAS DE ALQUILER DE COCHES
AGENCES DE LOCATION DE VOITURES
CAR RENTALS
AUTOVERMIETUNG

VIAJES MELIA. José Antonio, 29. Telf. 21 34 50.
HERTZ. Alemanes, 13. Telf. 21 39 76.
ROCAS. Hernando Colón, 30. Telf. 21 79 73.
ATESA. Queipo de Llano, 5. Telf. 21 41 93.
AVIS. Martín Villa, 6. Telf. 21 53 70.
ITAL. Queipo de Llano, 46. Telf. 21 30 99.

Aero-Taxis

ROCAS. Hernando Colón, 30. Telf. 21 79 73.

COMUNICACIONES
COMMUNICATIONS
COMMUNICATIONS
VERKEHRSVERBINDUNGEN

Ferrocarriles
Chemin de fer
Trains
Eisenbahn

Líneas a Madrid, Cádiz, Málaga, Granada, Huelva, Ayamonte, Mérida, Badajoz, Cáceres, Salamanca, Valencia y Barcelona.
RENFE (4). Información y venta anticipada de billetes. Martín Villa, 5. Telf. 22 89 94.

ESTACION DE CORDOBA. Plaza de Armas. Telf. 22 88 17.
ESTACION DE CADIZ. San Bernardo. Telf. 23 22 55.

Autobuses—Autobus Buses—Omnibusse

Líneas regulares a Córdoba, Granada, Málaga, Huelva, Ayamonte, Jerez, Cádiz, Badajoz, Cáceres-Salamanca-Valladolid, Lisboa, Ronda, Algeciras, La Línea, Albacete, Valencia, Arcos de la Frontera, Sanlúcar, Chipiona y Cabra-Lucena.
ESTACION DE AUTOBUSES. José María Osborne. Telf. 23 22 10. Todas las líneas excepto Huelva y Badajoz.
LINEA DE HUELVA. Empresa Damas Segura, 18. Telf. 22 22 72.
LINEA DE BADAJOZ. La Estellesa. Adriano, 36. Telf. 22 58 20.

Líneas aéreas—Lignes aériennes Air lines—Fluggesellschaften

Vuelos a Madrid, Lisboa, Valencia, Barcelona, Las Palmas, Tenerife, Tetuán, Casablanca, Tánger y Málaga y conexión con líneas aéreas extranjeras.
Reservas: Terminal Iberia. Almirante Lobo, 3. Telf. 22 89 01.
Aeropuerto de San Pablo: a 12 Kms. de la capital, en la carretera de Carmona.
Iberia representa todas las compañías extranjeras en Sevilla.

Líneas marítimas Lignes maritimes Maritime lines Schiffahrtsgesellschaften

COMPAÑIA TRASMEDITERRANEA. San Fernando, 9. Telf. 21 78 05.
IBARRA Y COMPAÑIA, S. A. Menéndez Pelayo, 2. Telf. 23 23 00. Informes: Joaquín de Haro. Tomás de Ibarra, 7. Telf. 22 12 02.
COMPAÑIA TRASATLANTICA. Rafael González Abréu, 5. Telf. 22 33 40.
AMERICAN EXPORT LINES. Plaza Nueva, 5. Telf. 22 28 99-8.
EMILIO HUART. Plaza Nueva, 5. Telf. 21 81 02.
AGENCIA CONCORDIA LINES. Edificio Elcano. Avenida Raza. Telf. 23 48 11.
NAVIERA CONDAL, S. A. Informes: Vda. de Filomeno de Aspe. Santo Tomás, 17. Telfs. 22 54 66 y 22 75 16.
MAC ANDREWS LINE. Plaza Calvo Sotelo, 5. Telf. 22 67 75-6.

TAXIS Paradas Arrêts—Stops Halteplätze

Queipo de Llano. Telf. 22 00 88.
Alemanes. Telf. 22 95 78.
Martín Villa. Telf. 22 74 87.
Puerta Jerez. Telf. 22 53 95.
Plaza Nueva.
Plaza del Salvador.
Marqués de Paradas. Telf. 22 22 80.
Altozano. Telf. 33 46 39.
Macarena. Telf. 37 18 90.
Puerta Osario. Telf. 25 85 42.
Luis Montoto. Telf. 25 43 24.
Borbolla. Telf. 23 40 61.
Moliní. Telf. 23 47 43.
Heliópolis. Telf. 31 04 46.
Virgen de Luján. Telf. 27 11 06.
Plaza del Duque. Telf. 21 42 21.
Plaza del Salvador.

TALLERES DE REPARACION DE AUTOMOVILES ATELIERS DE REPARATION D'AUTOMOBILES AUTO REPAIR GARAGES AUTOREPARATURWERKSTÄTTEN

SEIDA. Carretera de Carmona, 6. Telf. 35 06 00. Especialidad autos de grupo inglés y Volkswägen.
SERVICIO OFICIAL SEAT, FIAT. Gonzalo Bilbao, 29. Telf. 25 13 00.
GRUPO RENAULT. Carretera de Su Eminencia. Telf. 31 04 50.
GRUPO CITROEN. Luis Montoto, 30. Telfs. 25 44 35 y 25 82 19 (taller).
GENERAL MOTORS. Almadén de la Plata, 12. Telf. 35 46 93.
GRUPO PEUGEOT. Padre Méndez Casariego, 19. Telf. 25 13 07.
AUSTIN Y MORRIS. Sánchez Perrier, 1. Telf. 37 11 97.
MERCEDES BENZ, VOLKSWAGEN, DKW. Autopista de S. Pablo. Telf. 25 87 00.

ESTACIONES DE SERVICIO STATIONS DE SERVICE SERVICE STATIONS TANKSTELLEN

SEVILLA. Carretera Dos Hermanas (Avenida Reina Victoria).
SEVILLA. Carretera Madrid-Cádiz, Km. 536,7.
SEVILLA. C/. Castilla, 131.
SEVILLA. C/. Oriente, 74.
SEVILLA. Carretera Sevilla-Granada, Km. 5,7.
SEVILLA. Avenida Moliní.
SEVILLA. Carretera Madrid-Cádiz, Km. 549,7.
SEVILLA. Ronda de Capuchinos.

ALCALA DE GUADAIRA. Carretera Sevilla-Málaga, Km. 15,1.
ALCALA DE GUADAIRA. Carretera Sevilla-Málaga, Km. 15 (desviación).
ALCOLEA DEL RIO. Carretera Córdoba-Sevilla, Km. 90,3.
LA ALGABA. Carretera Santiponce-La Algaba, Km. 3,2.
EL ARAHAL. Carretera Sevilla-Granada, Km. 44,3.
LAS CABEZAS DE SAN JUAN. Carretera Madrid-Cádiz, Km. 595,8.
LA CAMPANA. Carretera La Campana-Lora del Río, Km. 1,2.
CARMONA. Carretera Madrid-Cádiz, Km. 507,6.
CARMONA. Carretera Madrid-Cádiz, Km. 511,3.
CASTILLEJA DE LA CUESTA. Carretera Madrid-Huelva, Km. 553,8.
CAZALLA DE LA SIERRA. Carretera Cazalla-Lora del Río, Km. 0,2.
CONSTANTINA. Carretera Llerena-Utrera, por Carmona, Km. 22.
CORIA DEL RIO. Carretera Sevilla-Coria del Río, Km. 13,5.
EL CORONIL. Carretera Utrera-Villamartín, Km. 17.
DOS HERMANAS. Carretera Madrid-Cádiz, Km. 557.
DOS HERMANAS. Carretera Madrid-Cádiz, Km. 554,3.
ECIJA. Carretera Madrid-Cádiz, Km. 455,5.
ECIJA. Carretera Madrid-Cádiz, Km. 452.
ECIJA. Carretera Madrid-Cádiz, Km. 456,4.
ESTEPA. Carretera Sevilla-Málaga, Km. 109,5.
FUENTES DE ANDALUCIA. Carretera La Campana-Fuentes, Km. 15.
GINES. Carretera Madrid-Huelva, Km. 558,6.
LANTEJUELA. Carretera Fuentes de Andalucía-Osuna, Km. 20,1.
LEBRIJA. Carretera Madrid-Cádiz, Km. 613,7.
LEBRIJA. Carretera Utrera-Chipiona.
LORA DEL RIO. Carretera Carmona-Constantina, Km. 76,2.
LA LUISIANA. Carretera Madrid-Cádiz, Km. 471,2.
MARCHENA. Carretera Ecija-Jerez, Km. 37,3.
MARINALEDA. Carretera Ecija-La Roda, Km. 36,6.
MORON DE LA FRONTERA. C/. Vereda de los Caballeros, s/n.
OSUNA. Carretera Sevilla-Granada, Km. 86,4.
OSUNA. Carretera Ecija-Olvera, Km. 34,2.
LOS PALACIOS. Carretera Madrid-Cádiz, Km. 568,8.
PARADAS. Conf. Calles Velázquez y Turina.
PEÑAFLOR. Carretera Córdoba-Sevilla, Km. 63,6.
PUEBLA DEL RIO. Carretera Puebla a Villafranca, Km. 2,2.
LA RINCONADA. Carretera Sevilla-Lora del Río.
LA RODA DE ANDALUCIA. Carretera Sevilla-Granada, Km. 125,8.
SANLUCAR LA MAYOR. Carretera Madrid-Huelva, Km. 568,7.
SANTIPONCE. Carretera Salamanca-Sevilla, Km. 531,8.
UTRERA. Carretera Madrid-Cádiz, Km. 552,6.
UTRERA. Carretera Ecija-Jerez, Km. 75,6.
VALENCINA DE LA CONCEPCION. Carretera Mérida-Sevilla, Km. 533,5.
VILLA FRANCO DEL GUADALQUIVIR. Carretera Puebla del Río-Isla Mayor, Km. 22,7.
VILLAVERDE DEL RIO. Carretera Carmona-Villaverde, Km. 29.
EL VISO DEL ALCOR. Calle Avenida de Cristo Rey, s/n.

TEATROS Y CINES
THEATRES ET CINEMAS
THEATERS AND MOVIES
THEATER UND KINOS

TEATRO SAN FERNANDO. Tetuán, 12. Telf. 21 12 23.
TEATRO ALVAREZ QUINTERO. Laraña, 4. Telf. 22 02 39.
TEATRO CERVANTES. Amor de Dios, 25. Telf. 22 62 17.
ALVAREZ QUINTERO. Laraña, 4. Telf. 22 23 38.
ANDALUCIA. Ronda de Capuchinos. Telf. 35 15 87.
APOLO. Bustos Tavera, 11. Telf. 21 75 79.
CERVANTES. Amor de Dios, 25. Telf. 22 62 17.
COLISEO. Queipo de Llano, 46. Telf. 22 16 36.
FLORIDA. Menéndez Pelayo, 51. Telf. 25 26 16.
IMPERIAL. Sierpes, 37. Telf. 22 68 78.
LOS REMEDIOS. Asunción, 1. Telf. 27 20 24.
LLORENS. Rioja, 8. Telf. 22 68 28.
PALACIO CENTRAL. Caravaca, 4. Telf. 22 55 53.
PATHE. Cuna, 11. Telf. 22 34 90.
RIALTO. Padre J. de Córdoba, 22 y 24. Telf. 22 87 68.
VILLASIS. Martín Villa, 6. Telf. 22 94 92.

TABLAOS FLAMENCOS
SPECTACLES FLAMENCOS
FLAMENCO DANCING
LOKALE MIT FLAMENCO—VORFÜHRUNGEN

TABLAO FLAMENCO. Lope de Rueda, 7.
LA PARRILLA DEL HOTEL CRISTINA. Jardines Cristina, s/n. Telf. 22 66 80.
EL PATIO ANDALUZ. Plaza del Duque, 4. Telf. 21 30 20.
LOS GALLOS. Plaza de Santa Cruz, 6. Telf. 21 31 98.
LA COCHERA. Menéndez Pelayo, 42. Telf. 25 90 62.

SALAS DE FIESTAS—CABARETS NIGHT CLUBS—NACHTCLUBS

LA PARRILLA. Hotel Cristina. Telf. 22 66 80.
PATIO ANDALUZ. Plaza del Duque, 4. Telf. 21 30 20.
EL OASIS. Avenida de García Morato. Telf. 27 56 13.
VISTA ALEGRE. Carretera de Alcalá. Telf. 25 11 24.
MARCELINO. (Continuación de la Palmera). Telf. 31 10 00.
ALAZAN CLUB. Juan Sebastián Elcano, 21. Telf. 27 51 99.
EL DRAGON ROJO. Betis (frente al bar El Puerto). Telf. 27 20 07.
TURIN. Asunción, 19. Telf. 27 21 27.
MESALIN'S CLUB. (Los Remedios). Padre Damián, 26. Telf. 27 21 51.
PARRILLA HOTEL RIO. Virgen de Luján, 18. Telf. 27 00 00.

CLUB Y SOCIEDADES DEPORTIVAS CLUBS ET SOCIÉTÉS SPORTIVES CLUBS AND SPORTS SOCIETIES SPORTVEREINE UND SPORTCLUBS

AEROCLUB. Tablada. Telf. 27 53 97.
CLUB PINEDA. Equitación y Golf en Avenida de Jerez. Telf. 31 14 00.
BETIS TENIS CLUB. Calle San Salvador. Telf. 23 36 22.
CLUB TIRO DE PICHON. «El Carambolo». Telf. 330-400 (en Camas).
CLUB KADOKAN JUDO. Campamento, 55. Telf. 25 90 31.
CLUB NATACION SEVILLA. Trastamara, 15. Telfs. 21 21 80 y 21 40 64.
CLUB NAUTICO SEVILLA. Río Guadalquivir. Pte. Tablada. Telf. 27 65 05.
CLUB DE PESCA DEPORTIVA SAN RAFAEL. Calle Lepanto, 3. Telf. 22 80 42.
SOCIEDAD DEPORTIVA DE CAZA. García de Vinuesa, 2 y 4. Telf. 22 86 89.
CLUB TAURINO (MUSEO TAURINO). Plaza de la Encarnación, 25. Telf. 21 40 54.
REAL AUTOMOVIL CLUB DE ANDALUCIA. Avenida de José Antonio, 14. Telf. 22 13 02.
REAL MOTO CLUB DE ANDALUCIA. Federico Sánchez Bedoya. Telf. 21 55 02.
MUTUA NACIONAL DEL AUTOMOVIL. Adolfo Rodríguez Jurado, 16. Telf. 21 18 30 y 21 56 53.
TOURING CLUB. Adolfo Rodríguez Jurado, 16. Telf. 21 18 30.
NEGOCIADO DE DEPORTES DEL AYUNTAMIENTO. Telf. 22 59 99.
JUNTA PROVINCIAL DE EDUCACION FISICA Y DEPORTES. Sales y Ferrer, 16. Telf. 22 47 50.
CLUB LYONS. Residencia oficial: Hotel Alfonso XIII. Secretaría oficial: señorita Charito Vázquez. Telf. 22 22 02.
DINNERS CLUB. Representante en Sevilla don Fernando Aguilar. Virgen de la Estrella, 11. Telf. 27 31 95.
SKAL CLUB. Alemanes, 3. Telf. 21 31 33.
CLUB ANDALUCIA «KARATE-JUDO». Calle Tomillo, 9.

GUIAS Y GUIAS INTERPRETES GUIDES ET GUIDES INTERPRETES GUIDES AND INTERPRETORS FREMDENFÜHRER UND DOLMETSCHER

OFICINA MUNICIPAL DE TURISMO (Reales Alcázares) (9). Telf. 22 95 74.

CONSULADOS—CONSULATS CONSULATES—KONSULATE

REPUBLICA FEDERAL ALEMANA. F. Sánchez Bedoya, 12. Telf. 21 55 20.
BELGICA. M. Siurot, 30. Telfs. 25 81 00 (particular), 31 14 48 (oficina).
BOLIVIA. Amor de Dios, 6. Telf. 22 69 42.
BRASIL. Valparaiso, 20. Telf. 23 26 45.
COLOMBIA. Pabellón de Colombia. Avenida de Moliní. Telf. 23 35 01.
CHILE. La Rábida, 3. Telf. 23 12 93.
REPUBLICA DE COSTA RICA. Julio César, 2. Telfs. 22 78 41 (oficina) y 22 66 27 (particular).
REPUBLICA DE CUBA. Pabellón de Cuba. Avenida Victoria, 22. Telf. 23 25 55.
DINAMARCA. Paseo de Delicias, 3. Telf. 22 09 17.
REPUBLICA DOMINICANA. Avenida Manuel Siurot, 3. Telf. 23 47 53.
EL SALVADOR. Canalejas, 5. Telf. 22 06 52.
ESTADOS UNIDOS. Pabellón de Estados Unidos. Paseo de las Delicias. Telf. 23 18 85.
FRANCIA. Plaza de Santa Cruz, 1. Telfs. 22 28 97 (oficina) y 22 28 96 (particular).
FINLANDIA. Santa Elena, 6. Villa Argentina. Telfs. 25 48 11 y 22 51 74 (particular).
GRECIA. Carretera de Carmona, 11. Telf. 35 35 00.
GRAN BRETAÑA. Méndez Núñez, 21. Telfs. 22 88 75-4-3.
GUATEMALA. Lara, 1. Telf. 25 71 04.
HONDURAS. Paseo de Cristóbal Colón, 13. Telf. 22 86 92.
HOLANDA (PAISES BAJOS). Cuna, 1. Telf. 22 99 52.
ITALIA. Bailén, 34. Telf. 22 24 40.
LIBERIA. Avenida de la Raza, Apto. 15, C. Telfs. 23 44 44 (oficina) y 22 86 92 (particular).
MONACO. Cristóbal Morales, 5. Telf. 22 05 25.
NICARAGUA. San Miguel, 4. Telf. 22 78 23.

NORUEGA. Antonio Maura, 1. Tabladilla. Telf. 23 25 93.

REPUBLICA DE PANAMA. Arjona, 19. Apartamento, 14. Telf. 21 17 33.

PERU. Pabellón del Perú. Avenida María Luisa. Telf. 23 28 19.

PORTUGAL. Pabellón de Portugal. Avenida del Cid. Telf. 23 11 50.

SUIZA. Paseo Calvo Sotelo, 3. Telf. 22 15 80.

SUECIA. Paseo de las Delicias, 2. Telfs. 29 09 15-16-17.

URUGUAY. Avenida Espinosa y Carcel, 86. Telf. 25 10 05.

VENEZUELA. Juan Pablo, 1. Telf. 23 21 42.

FILIPINAS. Alvareda, 1. Telf. 21 78 21.

BANCOS—BANQUES BANKS—BANKEN

BANCO ANDALUCIA. Rioja, 9. Telf. 22 59 80.

BANCO DE BILBAO. Granada, 6. Telf. 22 66 35.

BANCO CENTRAL. Avenida de José Antonio, 3. Telf. 22 48 20.

BANCO COCA, S. A. Tetuán, 35. Telf. 22 88 24.

BANCO COMERCIAL TRANSATLANTICO. Avenida de José Antonio, 7. Telf. 22 67 10-1.

BANCO DE ESPAÑA. Pl. Falange Española, 16. Telf. 22 66 50.

BANCO ESPAÑOL DE CREDITO. J. Guichot, 1. Telf. 22 49 25.

BANCO EXTERIOR DE ESPAÑA. Rioja, 26. Telf. 22 29 03.

BANCO HIPOTECARIO DE ESPAÑA. Avenida Queipo de Llano, 48. Telf. 22 48 07.

BANCO HISPANO AMERICANO. Sierpes, 91-93-95. Telf. 22 49 45.

BANCO DE LONDRES Y AMERICA DEL SUR. Ltdo. Plaza Nueva, 21. Telfs. 22 29 97-6-5.

BANCO DE MADRID. Albareda, 2-4. Telfs. 21 79 91-2.

BANCO MERCANTIL E INDUSTRIAL. Sierpes, 24. Telf. 22 67 33.

BANCO RURAL Y MEDITERRANEO. Cerrajería, 18. Telf. 22 48 70.

BANCO DE SANTANDER. Tetuán, 16. Telf. 22 89 91.

BANCO DE SEVILLA, S. A. Plaza Nueva, 7. Telf. 22 49 50.

BANCO URQUIJO. José Antonio, 10. Telfs. 22 09 01 y 22 86 42.

BANCO DE VIZCAYA. Sierpes, 87. Telf. 22 67 02.

BANCO ZARAGOZANO. Sierpes, 59. Telf. 22 29 83.

BANCO GENERAL COMERCIAL INDUSTRIAL. Plaza Nueva, 14. Telf. 21 80 30.

Cambio de divisas:

Bancos, Agencias de Viajes, Hoteles de Lujo y 1.ª categoría.

BIBLIOTECAS—BIBLIOTHÉQUES LIBRARIES—BIBLIOTHEKEN

BIBLIOTECA Y ARCHIVO MUNICIPAL. Ayuntamiento.

BIBLIOTECA PROVINCIAL. Universidad.

BIBLIOTECA PUBLICA. Rioja, 25.

ARCHIVO DE INDIAS. (Para Investigadores).

BIBLIOTECA ESCUELA DE ESTUDIOS HISPANO-AMERICANOS. Alfonso XII, 12.

BIBLIOTECA CAPITULAR - COLOMBINA. Entrada por el Patio de los Naranjos.

BIBLIOTECA DE LAS DISTINTAS FACULTADES. En la Universidad.

HEMEROTECA. Pabellón Mudéjar de la Plaza de América.

ARTE Y ARTESANIA ART ET ARTISANAT ART AND CRAFTS KUNSTGEWERBE

MANTILLAS Y VELOS. M. Adarve. Plaza Alfaro, 4. Telf. 22 00 67.

BORDADOS ARTESANIA. Plaza Doña Elvira, 4. A. Osuna. Telf. 21 47 48.

FABRICA DE MANTONES Y MANTILLAS. Luciano Foronda. Alvarez Quintero, 76. Telf. 22 91 48.

TRAJES DE FLAMENCA. Pardales. Calle Cuna, 19. Telf. 21 37 09.

FABRICA DE MANTONES, ARTESANIA TEXTIL. García de Vinuesa, 37. Telf. 22 01 25.

FABRICA DE PEINETAS. Rom-Val. Calle Pajaritos, 5. Telf. 22 77 62.

FABRICA DE ABANICOS. Casa Rubio. Sierpes, 66. Telf. 22 68 72.

TALLER DE BORDADO PARA IMAGENES. Guillermo Carrasquilla. Calle San Luis, 36. Telf. 22 36 20.

FABRICANTE DE CASTAÑUELAS Y GUITARRAS «FILIGRANA». Cereza, 9 (Bda. Carmen).

TALLER DE ORFEBRERIA. Seco-Velasco. Matahacas, 14. Telf. 25 13 28.

TALLER DE CERRAJERIA. José Avila. Campo de los Mártires, 7. Telf. 25 56 21.

TALLER DE ORFEBRERIA. M. Marmolejo. Baños, 43. Telf. 22 34 39.

TALLER DE BORDADO EN ORO Y TRAJES DE TORERO. «Manfredi». Toneleros, 3. Telf. 22 46 22.

Fábricas de Cerámicas Fabriques de Ceramiques Ceramic Factories Keramikfabriken

CERAMICA SANTA ANA. San Jorge, 31.

CERAMICA SEVILLA. Pimienta, 9.

LA CARTUJA. (Pickman, S. A.). A 3 Kms.

CERAMICA MONTALBAN. Alfarería, 11.

MENSAQUE RODRIGUEZ Y CIA. Evangelista, 47.
RAMOS REJANO. San Jacinto, 101.

Anticuarios
Antiquaires
Antique shops
Antiquitäten

J. A. CASTILLO. Plaza de Sta. Marta, 3. Telf. 22 80 05.
ALBERTO LINARES. Mateos Gago, 3. Telf. 22 21 45.
M. ORTEGA GOMEZ. José Antonio, 5. Telf. 22 33 45.
F. PIÑARES. Hernando Colón, 45. Telf. 22 32 00.
C. MORO. Placentines, 20. Telf. 22 46 33.
A. LINARES MUÑOZ. Alvarez Quintero, 90. Telf. 22 20 19.
M. ADARVE LINARES. Santo Tomás, 1. Telf. 22 52 16.

TRANSPORTES INTERNACIONALES
TRANSPORTS INTERNATIONAUX
INTERNATIONAL TRANSPORTS
INTERNATIONALE TRANSPORTE

Federico Mitchel. Hernando Colón.

FIESTAS POPULARES

SEMANA SANTA. Procesiones en Sevilla, desde el Domingo de Ramos hasta el Sábado Santo, por las tardes, y el Viernes Santo, de madrugada. La carrera oficial para todas las procesiones comprende la Campana, Sierpes, Plaza de Falange y Avenida de José Antonio, hasta la Catedral. La Semana Santa reviste también gran importancia y notables peculiaridades en Carmona, Osuna, Ecija, Estepa y Lebrija.
CASTILLEJA DE LA CUESTA. Procesiones del Domingo de Resurrección, con la vuelta «Rociera».
FERIA DE ABRIL. Tradicionalmente se celebra del 18 al 23, pudiendo retrasarse si la Semana Santa cae en estas fechas o se halla inmediata, para que medie un intervalo de 8 a 10 días. No se hace nunca programa, excepto para las corridas de toros. La estampa colorista más bella de España.
ROMERIA DEL ROCIO. Se celebra en el Santuario del Rocío, en Almonte (Huelva), el Domingo de Pentecostés. Las carretas, pertenecientes a las dos hermandades de Sevilla (San Jacinto y El Salvador), salen en la mañana del jueves anterior a Pentecostés y regresan el miércoles (El Salvador), y el jueves (San Jacinto) siguientes. Las ceremonias religiosas se celebran en el Santuario el domingo y el lunes por l mañana. Baile de sevillanas, ambiente es pecial, cuadro folklórico único.
CORPUS CHRISTI. Procesión a las 8 d la mañana con la Custodia de Arfe. Bail de los «Seises» en la Catedral durante l Octava. Los «Seises», bailan también e la Octava de la Purísima (diciembre) y e domingo, lunes y martes de Carnaval.
CORRIDAS DE TOROS Y MERCADO GANADERO. Ultimos días de septiembre (su pervivencia de la Antigua Feria de Sa Miguel).
FESTIVALES DE ESPAÑA. 2.ª quincena d septiembre.
ROMERIA AL SANTUARIO DE CONSOLACION. Utrera, 8 de septiembre.
ROMERIA DEL VALME. Dos Hermanas. Tercer domingo de octubre.
ROMERIA AL SANTUARIO DE CUATROVITAS. Bollullos de la Mitación. Cuart domingo de octubre.
FERIAS Y CERTAMENES. Feria de Muestra Ibero-Americana. Del 15 al 30 de abr (1967).

FETES POPULAIRES

SEMAINE SAINTE. Processions à Sévill depuis le Dimanche de Rameaux jusqu'a Samedi Saint, l'après-midi, et du Vendred Saint, le matin. Le parcours officiel pou toutes les processions comprend la Campana, Sierpes, Plaza de Falange et Avd. de José Antonio jusqu'à la Cathédrale. L Semaine Sainte a aussi une grande importance et des particularités remarquables Carmona, Osuna, Ecija, Estepa et Lebrij.
CASTILLEJA DE LA CUESTA. Procession d Dimanche de Résurrection avec la «vuel Rociera».
FOIRE D'AVRIL. Se célèbre traditionnelleme du 18 au 23 mais peut être retardé si Semaine Sainte coïncide avec ces dates o est toute proche, pour qu'il y ait un interval de 8 à 10 jours. On ne fait jamais de programme, sauf pour les corridas. La plu belle estampe coloriste d'Espagne.
ROMERIA DEL ROCIO. A lieu au Sanctuai du Rocio à Almonte (Huelva) le dimanch de Pentecôte. Les chariots, appartenant au deux confréries de Séville (Saint Jacint et El Salvador) partent le matin du jeu antérieur à la Pentecôte et reviennent mercredi (El Salvador) et jeudi (S. Jacinto suivants. Les cérémonies religeuses son célébrées au Sanctuaire le dimanche et lundi matin. Danse de sévillanes, ambianc spéciale, tableau folklorique unique.
CORPUS CHRISTI (Fête-Dieu). Processio à 8 h. du matin avec l'Ostensoir d'Arf Danse des «Seises» dans la Cathédra pendant l'Octave. Les «Seises» dansent aus

à l'Octave de la Très Pure (décembre) et les dimanche, lundi et mardi de Carnaval.

CORRIDAS DE TAUREAUX ET MARCHE AU BETAIL. Derniers jours de septembre (survivance de l'Ancienne Foire de St. Michel).

FESTIVALS D'ESPAGNE. 2.ª quinzaine de septembre.

PELERINAGE AU SANCTUAIRE DE CONSOLATION. Utrera, 8 septembre.

PELERINAGE DU VALME. Dos Hermanas, troisième dimanche d'octobre.

PELERINAGE AU SANCTUAIRE DE CUATROVITAS. Bollullos de la Mitación 4è dimanche d'octobre.

FOIRES ET CONCOURS. Foire commerciale ibéro-américaine. Du 15 au 30 avril (1967).

POPULAR HOLIDAYS

HOLY WEEK. Processions in Seville, from Palm Sunday to Holy Saturday, in the afternoons and on Good Friday, from dawn. The official route for the procession includes la Campana, Sierpes, Plaza de Falange and Avenida de José Antonio, to the Cathedral.

Holy Week celebrations are also important and interesting in Carmona, Osuna, Ecija, Estepa and Lebrija.

CASTILLEJA DE LA CUESTA. Processions on Easter Sunday with the «Rociera».

APRIL FAIR. Traditionally celebrated from the 18 to the 23, or a little later if Holy Week falls during this time or within 8 to 10 days. There is no established program except for the bull fights. The most beautiful, colorful spectacle in Spain.

PILGRIMAGE OF THE ROCIO. Celebrated in the Sanctuary of the Rocio, in Almonte (Huelva), on Pentecost Sunday. The processions, belonging to the two brotherhoods of Seville (San Jacinto and El Salvador) leave on the Thursday before Pentecost in the morning and return the following Wednesday (El Salvador) and Thursday (San Jacinto). The religious ceremonies are held in the sanctuary on Sunday and Monday in the morning. Sevillana dancing, special atmosphere, unique folkloric setting.

CORPUS CHRISTI. Procession at 8 in the morning with the Monstrance by Arfe. Dance of the «Seises» in the Cathedral during the Octava. The «Seises» also dance in the Octava of the Purísima (December) and on Sunday, Monday and Tuesday of Carnaval.

BULL FIGHTS AND LIVESTOCK MARKET. Last days of September (The remains of the old Fair of San Miguel).

FESTIVALS OF SPAIN. Second fifteen days of September.

PILGRIMAGE TO THE SANCTUARY OF CONSOLACION. Utrera. September 8.

PILGRIMAGE OF THE VALME. Dos Hermanas. Third Sunday in October.

PILGRIMAGE TO THE SANCTUARY OF CUATRO VITAS. Bollullos de la Mitación. Fourth Sunday in October.

FAIRS AND CONTESTS. Ibero-American Fair. From April 15 to April 30 (1967).

VOLKSFESTE

KARWOCHE. Prozessionen in Sevilla von Palmsonntag bis Karsamstag jeden Abend; Karfreitag bei Tagesanbruch. Die offiizielle Wegstrecke für alle Prozessionen führt durch die Strassen Campana, Sierpes, Plaza de Falange und Avenida de José Antonio bis zur Kathedrale.

Ebenfalls von grosser Bedeutung ist die Karwoche in Carmona, Osuna, Ecija, Estepa und Lebrija.

CASTILLEJA DE LA CUESTA. Prozessionen am Ostersonntag.

FERIA IM APRIL. Traditionsgemäss feiert man die Feria vom 18.—23. April. Fällt das Osterfest in diese Zeit, wird sie verschoben, damit immer eine Zeitspanne von 8—10 Tagen zwischen den beiden Festen liegt. Es werden nie Programme, bis auf die für die Stierkämpfe, gedruckt. Das schönste und bunteste Schauspiel Spaniens.

ROMERIA DEL ROCIO. Diese Wallfahrt feiert man am Pfingstsonntag im Sanktuarium del Rocío in Almonte (Huelva). Die den zwei Bruderschaften (San Jacinto und El Salvador) aus Sevilla gehörenden Karren brechen am Donnerstag abend vor dem Pfingstfest auf und kehren am folgenden Mittwoch (El Salvador) und Donnerstag (San Jacinto) wieder zurück. Die religiösen Zeremonien werden am Sonntag und Montag morgen im Sanktuarium abgehalten. Man tanzt «sevillanas» und schaut den Volkstanzgruppen bei ihren Darbietungen zu.

FRONLEICHNAM. Morgens um 8.00 Uhr findet die Prozession mit der Monstranz von Arfe statt. Tanz der Chorknaben in den acht Tagen nach dem Fronleichnamsfest. Die Chorknaben, die sogenannten «Seises», tanzen auch in der Oktave nach Mariä Empfängnis (Dezember) und am Karnevalssonntag, —montag und— dienstag.

STIERKAMPFE UND VIEHMARKT. In den letzten Septembertagen.

FESTIVALES DE ESPAÑA (Spanische Festspiele). In der zweiten Septemberhälfte.

WALLFAHRT ZUM SANKTUARIUM DE CONSOLACION. Utrera. Findet am 8. September statt.

ROMERIA DEL VALME. Wallfahrt in Dos Hermanas am dritten Sonntag im Oktober.

WALLFAHRT ZUM SANKTUARIUM DE CUATROVITAS. Bollullos de la Mitación. Findet am vierten Sonntag im Oktober statt.

MESSEN UND WETTBEWERDE. Iberoamerikanische Mustermesse 15.—30. April (1967).

CAZA Y PESCA

CAZA. En toda la provincia es posible la caza menor, y la caza mayor en los pueblos de la sierra. Todos los cotos son particulares o de las Sociedades de Caza y Pesca locales, a los que puede recurrirse.

PESCA. Coto de Alcalá del Río, sobre el Guadalquivir. Especie principal: ciprínidos. Todo el año.

Coto de la Minilla, en el embalse del mismo nombre. Especie principal: ciprínidos y barbo. Todo el año.

Pantano del Pintado, Black-bass.

En el río Guadalquivir, desde Sevilla a la desembocadura, pueden pescarse las especies de sábalos y albures.

Coto truchero en la Ribera del Huéznar, Cazalla y San Nicolás del Puerto. En el Genil-Ecija, barbo y carpa todo el año.

La Jefatura Provincial de Caza y Pesca, en Sevilla: Virgen del Valle, 46. Telf. 27 38 02.

CHASSE ET PECHE

CHASSE. Dans toute la province il est possible de chasser le petit gibier et la chasse au gros gibier dans les villages de la sierra. Toutes les réserves sont particulières ou des Sociétés de Chasse et pêche locales, auxquelles on peut s'adresser.

PECHE. Réserve d'Alcalá del Río, sur le Guadalquivir. Espèce principale: cyprinidés. Toute l'année.

Coto de la Minilla, dans le barrage du même nom. Espèce principale: cyprinidés et barbeau. Toute l'année.

Barrage de Pintado: black-bass.

Dans le Guadalquivir, depuis Séville vers l'embouchure, on peut pêcher les aloses et cabots. Réserve de truites à la Ribera del Huéznar, Cazalla et San Nicolás del Puerto. A Genil-Ecija, barbeau et carpe toute l'année.

La Direction Provinciale de Chasse et Pêche à Séville: Virgen del Valle, 46. Telf. 27 38 02.

HUNTING AND FISHING

HUNTING. Small game hunting is possible is the entire province, and big game hunting in the mountain areas. All the preserves and areas are private or belong to the local Hunting and Fishing Societies, which can be contacted.

FISHING. Coto de Alcalá del Río, on the Guadalquivir. All year round: «ciprínidos».

Coto de la Minilla, at the dam of the same name. All year round: «ciprínidos» and barbel.

Pintado Dam, Black bass.

In the Guadalquivir River, from Seville to the outlet, there are shad and dace.

Trout fishing in the Ribera del Huéznar, Cazalla and San Nicolás del Puerto. In the Genil-Ecija, barbel and carp all year round.

The Provincial Chief of Hunting and Fishing, in Seville: Virgen del Valle, 46. Telf. 27 38 02.

JAGD UND FISCHFANG

JAGD. Niederjagd ist in der ganzen Provinz, Hochjagd in den Gebirgsdörern möglich. Alle Jagdgehege sind Privatbesitz oder gehören den jeweiligen örtlichen Jagdvereinen, an die man sich wenden kann.

FISCHFANG. Angeirevier Alcalá del Río am Guadalquivir. Hauptarten: Karpfenartige Fische, die man das ganze Jahr hindurch angeln kann.

Coto de la Minilla (Angelrevier) am Stausee gleichen Namens. Hauptarten: Karpfenartige Fische und Barben, die das ganze Jahr hindurch zu angeln sind.

Pantano del Pintado (Stauwerk): Forellen black-bass.

Im Guadalquivir kann man von Sevilla bis zur Mündung alle Arten von Alsen und Weissfischen angeln.

Forellengebiet in Ribera del Huéznar, Cazalla und San Nicolás del Puerto. In Genil-Ecija, das ganze Jahr hindurch Barben und Karpfen.

Jefatura Provincial de Caza y Pesca (Amt für Jagd und Fischfang) in Sevilla. Virgen del Valle 46. Telefon 27 38 02.

EXCURSIONES DE SEVILLA A LA PROVINCIA

Santiponce

A 9 Kms. de Sevilla por la carretera de Mérida. Existen dos monumentos nacionales de extraordinario interés histórico, artístico y arqueológico.

MONASTERIO DE SAN ISIDORO DEL CAMPO. Se encuentra a la entrada del pueblo. Fue fundado por Guzmán el Bueno. La iglesia contiene las estatuas orantes de los fundadores, obra de Martínez Montañés. El retablo del Altar Mayor es una obra maestra de Martínez Montañés.

RUINAS DE ITALICA. Están a 1,50 Kms. del pueblo. Colonia romana en la que nacieron los emperadores Trajano y Adriano. Se conservan restos de calles porticadas, un grandioso anfiteatro y maravillosos mosaicos.

San Juan de Aznalfarache

A 4 Kms. Monumento al Sagrado Corazón. Magnífica vista sobre Sevilla.

Alcalá de Guadaira

A 15 Kms. Castillo romano reformado por los árabes. Iglesia de la Virgen del Aguila. Maravillosos paisajes. Molinos antiguos utilizando la corriente del agua.

Ecija

A 86 Kms. «Ciudad de las Torres», con muchas e interesantes iglesias; mosaicos romanos en el Ayuntamiento; palacios señoriales, como el del Marqués de Peñaflor, con su famoso balcón corrido, el de los Duques de Benamejí, el de los Condes del Aguila y otros.

Carmona

A 32 Kms. Necrópolis; romana; Museo junto a la Necrópolis. Alcázar y puertas romanas, con modificaciones musulmanas. Iglesias mudéjares con importantes tesoros artísticos. Una de las ciudades andaluzas más importantes en tiempo de los árabes.

Osuna

A 86 Kms. Colegiata con magnifico Museo de Arte Sacro, que incluye lienzos de Ribera y una talla de la Virgen atribuida a Alonso Cano. Sepulcro de los Duques de Osuna (el patio de entrada es una verdadera joya del estilo plateresco) y antigua Universidad, hoy Instituto de Segunda Enseñanza. Magníficas casas-palacio con patios, como la del Marqués de la Gomera, puro colonial.

Marchena

A 60 Kms. Recinto amurallado almohade, conservado en su casi totalidad con una puerta de gran belleza llamada «Arco de la Rosa». Iglesia de San Juan. Convento de San Agustín (la iglesia tiene influencia azteca e incaica). Plaza de Armas del Palacio Ducal de Arcos. Casas señoriales con bellas portadas.

Estepa

A 110 Kms. Pueblo de empinadísimas calles. Conjunto de interesantes iglesias barrocas. Palacio de los Cerverales. Numerosas fábricas de polvorones y mantecados.

Morón de la Frontera

A 65 Kms. Iglesia de San Miguel. Iglesia de la Compañía de Jesús y Palacio de Miraflores. Importantes industrias.

Utrera

A 36 Kms. Santuario de Nuestra Señora de la Consolación. Iglesias de Santa María de la Asunción y de Santiago. Palacios de los Cuadra, hoy Ayuntamiento. Grandes industrias aceituneras.

Mairena del Alcor

A 18 Kms. Castillo con Museo de Jorge Bonsor que cuenta con lienzos de Valdés Leal y colección de piezas arqueológicas de todas las épocas especialmente romanas y también cerámica popular.

Lebrija

A 77 Kms. Iglesia de Santa María, con impresionante estatua de la Virgen de la Oliva, debida a Alonso Cano.

Bollullos de la Mitación

A 14 Kms. Santuario de Cuatrovitas (a 5 Kms. del pueblo), antigua mezquita almohade. Monumento Nacional.

Paradas

A 48 Kms. Cuadro de «La Magdalena» de El Greco, en la iglesia de San Eutropio.

Sierra Morena

El norte de la Provincia, constituye una zona de gran atractivo y belleza (Constantina, Cazalla) muy apropiada para verano. En término de El Ronquillo se hallan los «Lagos del Serrano» y el «Pantano de la Minilla», en cuyas márgenes van a ser construidas una urbanización y un complejo turístico respectivamente que, por su proximidad a la capital (41 Kms.), constituirán en el futuro una zona de vacaciones de la misma.

EXCURSIONS DE SEVILLE A LA PROVINCE

Santiponce

A 9 km. de Séville par la route de Mérida. Il existe deux monuments nationaux d'ex-

traordinaire intérêt historique, artistique et archéologique.

MONASTERE DE SAN ISIDORO DEL CAMPO. Se trouve à l'entrée du village. Fondé par Guzmán el Bueno. L'église contient les statues priantes des fondateurs, oeuvre de Martinez Montañés.

Le retable du maître autel est un chef d'oeuvre de Martinez Montañés.

RUINES D'ITALICA. Se trouvent à 1,50 km. du village. Colonie romaine ou naquirent les empereurs Trajan et Adrián. On conserve des restes de rues à portiques, un grandiose amphithéâtre et de merveilleuses mosaïques.

San Juan de Aznalfarache

A 4 km. Monument au Sacré Coeur. Magnifique vue de Séville.

Alcalá de Guadaira

A 15 km. Château romain réformé par les Arabes. Eglise de la Vierge de l'Aigle (del Aguila). Merveilleux paysages. Moulins antiques utilisant le courant de l'eau.

Ecija

A 86 km. «Ville des Tours» avec de nombreuses et intéressantes églises. Mosaïques romaines à l'Hôtel de Ville: palais seigneuriaux, comme celui du Marquis de Peñaflor, avec son fameux balcon-couloir, celui des Ducs de Benameji et celui des Comtes del Aguila et autres.

Carmona

A 32 km. Nécropole romaine. Musée à côté de la nécropole. Alcazar et portes romaines avec modifications musulmanes. Eglises mudéjares avec importants trésors artistiques. Une des villes andalouses les plus importantes au temps des Arabes.

Osuna

A 86 km. Collégiale avec magnifique musée d'Art Sacré qui contient des tableaux de Ribera et une statue de la Vierge atribuée à Alonso Cano. Sépulcre des Ducs d'Osuna (le patio d'entrée est un véritable joyau de style plateresque) et ancienne université, aujourd'hui Institut d'Enseignement Secondaire. Magnifiques maisons-palais avec patios, comme celle du Marquis de la Gomera pur colonial.

Marchena

A 60 km. Enceinte emmuraillée almohade conservée dans sa presque totalité avec une porte de grande beauté appelée «Arc de la Rosa». Eglise de St. Jean. Couvent de St. Augustin (l'église a une influence aztèque et inca). Plaze d'Armes du Palais Ducal de Arcos. Maisons seigneuriales avec beaux portiques.

Estepa

A 110 km. Village aux rues très escarpées. Ensemble d'intéressantes églises baroques. Palais des Cerverales. Nombreuses fabriques de polvorones et mantecados (bombons).

Morón de la Frontera

A 65 km. Eglise de St. Michel. Eglise de la Compagnie de Jésus et Palais de Miraflores. Importantes Industries.

Utrera

A 36 km. Sanctuaire de N. D. de la Consolation. Eglises de Ste. Marie de l'Assomption et de St. Jacques (Santiago). Palais des Cuadra, aujourd'hui Hôtel de Ville. Grandes industries de l'olive.

Mairena del Alcor

A 18 km. Château avec Musée de Jorge Bonsor qui contient des tableaux de Valdés Leal et collection de pièces archéologiques de toutes les époques spécialement romaine, et aussi céramique populaire.

Lebrija

A 77 km. Eglise de Ste. Marie avec impressionnante statue de la Vierge à l'Olive, due à Alonso Cano.

Bollullos de la Mitación

A 14 km. Sanctuaire de Cuatrovitas (à 5 km. du village) ancienne mosquée almohade. Monument National.

Paradas

A 48 km. Tableau de «La Magdalena» de El Greco, dans l'Eglise de San Eutropio.

Sierra Morena

Le nord de la Province constitue une zone de grand attrait et beauté (Constantina, Cazalla) très appropriée pour l'été. Sur le territoire de El Ronquillo se trouvent les «Lagos del Serrano» et le «Pantano de la Minilla» sur les bords desquels on va construire une urbanisation et un complexe touristique, respectivement, et qui, en raison de leur proximité de la capitale (41 km.) constitueront dans le futur une zone de vacances de celle-ci.

TOURS FROM SEVILLE TO THE PROVINCE

Santiponce

9 kilometers from Seville along the Mérida highway. Two national monuments of extraordinary historical, artistic and archaeological interest.

MONASTERY OF SAN ISIDORO DEL CAMPO. At the entrance to the town. Founded by Guzmán el Bueno. The church has the praying statues of the founders, by Martínez Montañés. The Main Altarpiece is a masterpiece by Martínez Montañés.

RUINS OF ITALICA. 1,5 kilometers from the town. Roman colony which was the birthplace of the emperors Trajano and Adriano. There are the remains of portico streets, a large amphitheater and marvelous mosaics.

San Juan de Aznalfarache

4 kilometers away. Monument to the Sacred Heart. Magnificent view of Seville.

Alcalá de Guadaira

15 kilometers away. Roman castle reformed by the Arabs. Church of the Virgen del Aguila. Marvelous views. Old wind mills at the stream.

Ecija

86 kilometers away. «City of the Towers», with many interesting churches; Roman mosaics in City Hall; Stately palaces, like the one of the Marquis of Peñaflor, with its famous balcony, the one of the Dukes of Benamejí, the one of the Counts of Aguila and others.

Carmona

32 kilometers away. Roman necropolis; and Museum. Fortress and Roman gates, with Moslem modifications. Christian-Moorish churches with important artistic treasures. One of the most important cities in Andalucía during the time of the Arabs.

Osuna

86 kilometers away. Colegiate church with magnificent Museum of Sacred Art, including canvases by Ribera and a carving of the Virgin attributed to Alonso Cano. Tomb of the Dukes of Osuna (the patio at the entrance is a true gem in Plateresque style) and the old University, today the Institute of Secondary Education. Magnificent palace-houses with patios, like the one of the Marquis of the Gomera, in pure colonial style.

Marchena

60 kilometers away. An almost complete Almohade Moorish walled enclosure with a very beautiful gate called «Arco de la Rosa». Church of San Juan. Convent of San Agustín (the church has Aztec and Inca influences). Plaza de Armas of the Palacio Ducal de Arcos. Stately houses with lovely entrances.

Estepa

110 kilometers away. Town with very steep streets. Group of very interesting Baroque churches. Palace of the Cerverales. Many «polvorones» and «mantecados» factories and bakeries.

Morón de la Frontera

65 kilometers away. Church of San Miguel. Church of the Company of Jesus and the Palace of Miraflores. Important industries.

Utrera

36 kilometers away. Sanctuary of Nuestra Señora de la Consolación. Churches of Santa María de la Asunción and of Santiago. Palaces of the Cuadra, today City Hall. Large olive industry.

Mairena del Alcor

18 kilometers away. Castle with Jorge Bonsor Museum, that contains canvases by Valdés Leal and a collection of Archaeological pieces from all periods, especially the Roman one and also popular ceramics.

Lebrija

77 kilometers away. Church of Santa María, with the moving statue of the Virgin of the Olive, attributed to Alonso Cano.

Bollullos de la Mitación

14 kilometers away. Sanctuary of Cuatrovitas (5 kil. from the town), an old Almohade Moorish mosque. National Monument.

Paradas

48 kilometers away. Painting of «La Magdalena» by El Greco in the church of San Eutropio.

Sierra Morena

In the North of the Province, a lovely area (Constantina, Cazalla), very good for summer. In the area around El Ronquillo, the «Lagos del Serrano» and the Dam of «la Minilla». On the banks, an urbanization and tourist complex that, because of their nearness to the capital (41 kil.), will be, in the future, a fine summer resort location.

AUSFLÜGE VON SEVILLA IN DIE PROVINZ

9 km von Sevilla entfernt befinden sich an der Landstrasse nach Mérida zwei Nationaldenkmäler von ausergewöhnlichen historischem, künstlerischem und archäologischen interesse.

KLOSTER SAN ISIDORO DEL CAMPO. An der Einfahrt ins Dorf befindet sich das von Guzmán el Bueno gegründete Kloster. Die Kirche enthält die betenden Statuen der Gründer, ein Werk von Martínez Montañés. Der Aufsatz des Hauptaltars ist ein Meisterwerk von Martínez Montañés.

RUINEN VON ITALICA. Befinden sich 1,50 km ausserhalb des Dorfes. Römische Kolonie, in der die Kaiser Trajan und Hadrian zur Welt kamen. Überreste von Strassen mit Säulengängen, vom Amphitheater und wunderschöne Mosaikarbeiten.

San Juan de Aznalfarache

4 km von Sevilla entfernt. Herzjesu-Denkmal. Herrlicher Blick auf Sevilla.

Alcalá de Guadaira

15 km von Sevilla entfernt. Römische Festung, die von den Arabern umgebaut wurde. Kirche der Virgen del Aguila. Schönes Landschaftsbild. Alte Wassermühlen.

Ecija

86 km von Sevilla entfernt liegt die «Stadt der Türme» mit ihren vielen interessanten Kirchen. Römische Mosaikarbeiten im Rathaus. Herrschaftliche Paläste wie der des Marqués de Peñaflor mit seinem berühmten Balkon, der der Herzöge von Benamejí, der Grafen del Aguila und andere mehr.

Carmona

32 km von Sevilla entfernt. Römische Nekropolis. Museum neben der Nekropolis. Römischer Alkazar und römische Tore, die von den Muselmanen neugestaltet wurden. Kirchen im Mudejarstil mit bedeutenden Kunstschätzen. Eine der wichtigsten andalusischen Städte aus der arabischen Zeit.

Osuna

86 km von Sevilla entfernt. Stiftskirche mit Museum, das Gemälde von Ribera und eine Muttergottesstatue von Alonso Cano enthält. Grabmal der Herzöge von Osuna (der Eingangshof ist ein wahrhaftiges Juwel des plateresken Stils). Alte Universität, heute Oberschule. Herrliche palastähnliche Häuser mit Innenhöfen, wie das des Marqués de la Gomera im Kolonialstil.

Marchena

60 km von Sevilla entfernt. Von den Almohaden erbaute Stadtmauer, die fast vollständig erhalten blieb und ein schönes Tor, genannt «Arco de la Rosa» besitzt. San-Juan-Kirche. San-Agustín-Kloster, bei dessen Kirche die Inkas und Azteken ihren Einfluss ausglichen Palastes de Arcos. Herrschaftshäuser mit schönen Portalen.

Estepa

110 km von Sevilla entfernt. Dorf mit stellen Strassen. Interessante barocke Kirchen. Palacio de los Cerverales. Zahlreiche Keksfabriken.

Morón de la Frontera

65 km von Sevilla entfernt. San-Miguel-Kirche des Jesuitenordens und Palacio de Miraflores. Bedeutende Industrien.

Utrera

36 km von Sevilla entfernt. Sanktuarium de Nuestra Señora de la Consolación. Kirchen Santa María de la Asunción und Santiago. Palacio de los Cuadra, heute Rathaus. Grosse olivenverarbeitende Fabriken.

Mairena del Alcor

18 km von Sevilla entfernt. Burg mit Museum von Jorge Bonsor, das über Gemälde von Valdés Leal und eine Sammlung alter Stücke aus allen Epochen, vor allem aus der römischen, und auch über Keramik verfügt.

Lebrija

77 km von Sevilla entfernt. Santa-Maria-Kirche mit einer eindrucksvollen Muttergottesstaute, genannt Virgen de la Oliva, ein Werk von Alonso Cano.

Bollullos de la Mitación

14 km von Sevilla entfernt. Sanktuarium de Cuatrovitas (5 km ausserhalb des Dorfes). Alte Moschee der Almohaden, heute Nationaldenkmal.

Paradas

48 km von Sevilla entfernt. Gemälde «La Magdalena» von El Greco in der Kirche San Eutropio.

Sierra Morena

Im Norden der Provinz bildet diese Gebirgskette eine anziehende und landschaftlich schöne Gegend (Constantina, Cazalla), die besonders im Sommer sehr beliebt ist. Im Gebiet von El Ronquillo befinden sich die Lagos del Serrano (Seen) und der Pantano de la Minilla (Stauwerk), an dessen Ufern eine Wohnkolonie und ein Touristenkomplex entstehen sollen. Da diese Zone in unmittelbarer Nähe Sevillas (41 km) liegt, wird sie bald ein beliebtes Feriengebiet darstellen.

DISTANCIAS KILOMETRICAS DESDE SEVILLA A:
DISTANCES KILOMETRIQUES DEPUIS SEVILLE A:
DISTANCE IN KILOMETERS FROM SEVILLA TO:
ENTFERNUNGEN IN KILOMETERN VON SEVILLA NACH:

Aeropuerto	10
Alcalá de Guadaira	14
Alicante	612
Barcelona	1.023
Bilbao	866
Cádiz	154
Carmona	33
Córdoba	155
Ecija	85
Gerona	1.123
Granada	258
Hamburgo	2.488
Huelva	94
Jaén	245
Jerez de la Frontera	100
La Coruña	948
Logroño	873
Londres	2.234
Lora del Río	50
Madrid	541
Málaga	225
Marchena	60
Morón de la Frontera	65
Osuna	80
Oviedo	793
Pamplona	952
París	1.838
Roma	2.463
San Sebastián	938
Santander	839
Santiponce	8
Soria	767
Tarragona	927
Utrera	32
Valencia	668
Zaragoza	863

INDICE

I RUTA SEVILLA-SANTIPONCE-LORA DEL RIO-SEVILLA
II RUTA SEVILLA-S. JUAN DE ANALFARACHE-S. LUCAR LA MAYOR
III RUTA SEVILLA-OSUNA-UTRERA-LAS CABEZAS-SEVILLA
IV RUTA SEVILLA-CARMONA-ECIJA
CAMPING
MONUMENTOS
RECURSOS TURISTICOS
COTO DE PESCA
RESES BRAVAS
34 km.
44 km.
49 km.
89 km.
77 km.
Sierra de Lora
Guadalcanal
HAMAPEGA
906
Cuevas de Santiago
Alanis
Cortijo Calcón
S. Nicolás del Puerto
El Cerro del Hierro
Sierra del Pimpollar
Pantano del Pintado
Sierra de la Grana
Loma de Almendrita
Cazalla de la Sierra
Sierra Padrona
Sierra Palma
Colonia de Galeón
Lomas del Moral
C. 421
C. 435
Srio. de la Virgen del Monte
C. 432
Las Naves de la Concepción
Ribera de Ciudadeja
746
GIBARRAYO
Constantina
Fabrica del Pedroso
La Quintera
El Aguila
Almadén de la Plata
Loma del Espárrago
Sierra del Cubillo
El Pedroso
C. 433
I
Pantano de Derivación
Casas de las Jarillas
Dehesa de Frías
Est. Los Labrados
Castillo de Mulba
Dehesa del Ventorrillo
La Puebla de los Infantes
Almenara
SAN CRISTOBAL
462
Las Francas
Las Monjas
Risco Blanco
Sierra de Fuente Lengua
El Ronquillo
Sierra Bajosa
Hacienda de los Melonares
Estación Ventas Quemadas
Sierra Traviesa
Parroso
Estación Arenillas
Cerro de Rilla
Aldea del Pez
Corcoja
Nra. Sra. de Villadiego
Peñaflor
Virgen de Setefillas
C. 431
EMBALSE DE LA CALA
Castilblanco de los Arroyos
Cerros Palmita
Viar
CEBRÓN
412
Villanueva de las Minas
Lora del Río
Est. El Priorato
Monasterio de la Merced
Calonge
Presa del Judío
Jurisdición de Fuente Palmera
Venta del Alto
Alcolea